THE COLONY COOKBOOK

THE COLONY COOKBOOK

by Gene Cavallero, Jr., and Ted James

The Bobbs-Merrill Company, Inc.
Indianapolis / New York

The Bobbs-Merrill Company, Inc.
Indianapolis · New York

To my father and all suffering restaurateurs

CONTENTS

INTRODUCTION

For over a half a century, the Colony Restaurant served classic French and Italian cuisine to distinguished clientele. And for the past five years or so, I have been toying with the idea of writing a book about our restaurant. My reasons are varied. First, of course, I would like my readers to be able to prepare some of our famous dishes at home. Keep in mind that the recipes contained in the final section of the book are *adaptations* of our famous dishes. It is impossible to follow the recipes that we used in our restaurant's kitchen in the home kitchen. The reasons for this will be obvious. To begin with, we had an abundance of raw materials to work with. Hundreds of spices, rare herbs, exotic vegetables and fruits, fresh game and fish from the far corners of the earth were always on hand. The ovens in our kitchen were much hotter than any home oven could ever be. We had all of the necessary kitchen equipment for preparing the most difficult of cuisine. Our kitchen staff alone numbered over fifty. My wife and I have tested all the recipes in this book in our kitchen in the country, and the dishes are reasonable approximations of what you might have eaten at the Colony.

Secondly, I would like the public to know a little about the history of a great restaurant—how it was started, its growing pains, its maturity, and the many anecdotes and incidents that evolved through the years.

Third, I would like to give advice on food, its preparation, and the purchase of equipment, as well as on wines, behavior, and ordering in restaurants. Many people do not understand some of the basic concepts of restaurant behavior. I hope this book will be of some use in these areas.

Fourth, and most important, I would like the public to get a truer picture of what the restaurant business really is. My regular customers who came in year in and year out understood that my job was not a glamorous one. Most people do not have the slightest inkling of what a restaurateur must go through every day of the year in his efforts to please his customers. I hope you will read the section on "Gripes" in Chapter Three, and take it in the spirit in which it is offered. I would like you to understand what the luxury-restaurant business is, and why we must charge ten dollars for something you can get for four dollars somewhere else. I would like you to understand why you should not be abusive to captains and waiters. When they do make mistakes, remember that they are only human. I would like you to learn to take their advice when ordering food and wines.

Remember, they may not know a thing about anything else but they do know how to serve you, cook for you, and advise you when it comes to this basic area of your life.

I would like the American public to become more comfortable in restaurants. Perhaps some of my comments will help people to enjoy themselves more when dining out.

Sincerely,
Gene Cavallero, Jr.

THE COLONY COOKBOOK

CHAPTER ONE

The Story of
the Colony Restaurant

The year was 1920. The world had just emerged from the war to end all wars, and the United States had the year before declared itself "irrevocably" dry with the Volstead Act. One hundred million Americans were reading about Sacco and Vanzetti and listening to KDKA Pittsburgh on Marconi's miracle invention, the radio. Scott Fitzgerald had immortalized the "lost generation" in *This Side of Paradise* and enthralled a public ravenous to read all about flaming youth, flappers, hip flasks, and raccoon coats. Sinclair Lewis had chronicled middle-class manners and morals in *Main Street,* and Edith Wharton had splattered the pages of *The Age of Innocence* with the wiles and ways of the rich.

New Yorkers were flocking to the New Amsterdam Theater to hear Marilyn Miller sing in the Jerome Kern hit musical *Sally,* and were motoring out to watch Man O' War win the Belmont and Preakness stakes.

Whistling "Japanese Sandman," "Margie," and Paul Whiteman's slide-whistle smashes, "Whispering" and "Avalon," the country went to the polls and elected Warren G. Harding President. The cry was "Back to Normalcy," but the action, quite conversely, ushered in the decade that has come to be called the madcap Roaring Twenties.

It was during that year that a New York City businessman named Sylvester Haberman bought a small piece of real estate at the southeast corner of Madison Avenue and 61st Street. Although the neighborhood had tone, the mélange of types who occupied the building could hardly have been labeled "up to snuff."

An eccentric old doctor named Burke practiced on the first floor, the entrance to his rarely visited offices fronting on 61st Street. Next door, on Madison Avenue, was a rather sleazy, déclassé bistro. On the second floor, above the doctor's office, was a disreputable gambling joint, and above that a stolidly private nursing home.

The bistro was pretentiously called the Colony and was owned by a man named Joe Pani. From the start the place had been a bust, rarely if ever breaking even, let alone making money. Frequented by two-bit gamblers and free-wheeling flappers off Madison Avenue who came in to eat and run, the place was like a morgue every night. If a gentleman entered alone, it was automatically assumed that he was stopping in for a drink on his way upstairs to the gambling joint. The thought that he might have come in to eat never entered anyone's mind. And further, if a man ap-

peared at the Colony with his "wife" or "girl," the classi-
fication was immediate and irrevocable.

The atmosphere and reputation couldn't have been
less likely to produce a successful restaurant, and Joe Pani
knew it. He was stuck with a turkey. In desperation he decided to redecorate, install a dance floor, and bring in a jazz
band. "Perhaps this would do it," he thought.

As a rule, restaurateurs are shrewd businessmen. They
conceal their plans for a long while, ruminate at great
length over them, and then invariably confide in the wrong
person. One day Joe Pani inquired of Ernest Cerutti, the
headwaiter, "What do you think of turning the Colony
into a night club with a couple of good acts, a jazz band,
dance floor, spotlights, and all that?"

Ernest (Esterino Umberto Giuseppe Antonioni) Cerutti was, needless to say, appalled at the idea. True, he was
a headwaiter, and although never possessed of the airs of a
grand duke, nonetheless he was a man of refined tastes.
Well traveled, he was a natural-born host and a cultivated
gastronome, and his manners and deportment were equal
to those of a British diplomat. Born near Lago Maggiore,
Ernest was one of a family of innkeepers. His father also
successfully operated a dozen officers' messes for the very
particular Italian Army.

The idea of a ripsnorting jazz band accompanying a
superb *poularde à l'estragon* or a flaming flapper dancing
the Black Bottom and singing "Whoopee" while a perfect
blanquette de veau à l'Indienne slowly cooled to inedibility
made him blanch. From the start, the gentleman had
strongly counted on the fact that the good food served at the
Colony would eventually bring in an appreciative clientele.
He had absolutely no desire to establish the reputation of a
restaurant in the wake of a brassy, earsplitting repeat
chorus in a jazz palace.

And further, he told Joe Pani just that. Pani hit the

roof. After all, he was the owner of the Colony; Cerutti was his headwaiter, and of course he ought to concur regardless of his personal feelings. Cerutti allowed that this perhaps was one phase of his profession that he had never learned. And when he realized that Pani was determined to see his idea through, Cerutti resigned, left the Colony, and was soon headwaiter at the "in" Astor-owned Knickerbocker.

However, before leaving he sat down with his captain of waiters and with his head chef. My father, Gene Cavallero, Sr., whom he had known since 1908 when both were captains at the London Savoy, was his captain; in 1920 he had sold a hot-dog stand in Westchester County to join Cerutti at the Colony. The principal chef, Alfred Hartmann, came from Alsace. Both immediately agreed with Cerutti's disdain for the night-club image, and vowed that they would one day acquire the place from Pani and establish it as a first-class restaurant.

There is little information available on the next year or two of the Colony's history, for Pani never did succeed in making it a popular night club. The struggle for mere existence continued, with my father promoted to the rank of manager. He tried to sift the wheat from the chaff, but there simply was no wheat to replace the chaff. Even two-bit tinhorns were welcomed if they could pay cash for dinner.

The gambling casino upstairs brought in some business, and in order to accommodate the members, the Colony kitchen stayed open until three or four in the morning. Despite the rather seedy nature of the late-night business, the Colony had to serve them in order to make ends meet. A dish of scrambled eggs, a bowl of onion soup, and a few highballs at least kept the doors open.

Members of the gambling club occasionally came downstairs to eat dinner in the restaurant. For example, Arnold Rothstein, the "real-estate" man who was later murdered, would sprint down the stairs for a sandwich and a glass of ginger ale in between time passed at the gambling tables. And what would this rich gambler leave for a tip? Ten cents. He was the worst tipper in the history of the restaurant. However, Rothstein was not completely remiss in the area of human kindness and generosity. One night, after having won over ten thousand dollars from a young member of one of the most distinguished families of New York, he followed the lad to the men's room, handed the money back to him, and said, "Let this be a lesson to you, son. Next time, don't gamble with professionals."

During the last days of the two-year Pani regime the Colony, strangely enough, began to get its head above water. The clientele had slowly grown to triple the original number. Many of New York's playboys found the clandestine atmosphere the perfect place to take their mistresses. Affairs were "safe" at the Colony. As time went by, these women began to come to the Colony alone. Realizing that money was occasionally short, my father was generous in extending credit. Curiously, it was very rare that the bills were not paid. His shrewd analysis of his customers' ability to pay or not to pay caused talk in town. Credit could always be had at the Colony *if* Gene senior knew and trusted you. "Charge it!" was a reality at the Colony.

Perhaps even more important than the credit factor was that the customers found the food superb. Alfred Hartmann, the executive chef, was a perfectionist when it came to the preparation of food. He would, in fact, throw out nine sauces that had been labored over for hours if he found a tenth more to his liking. And keep in mind that in those days Hartmann was not yet part owner of the restaurant. He was still working for Pani, on salary, an employee. The fruits of his efforts still wound up in Joe Pani's pocket.

Service was another aspect of the initial attention. Hartmann, together with my father, insisted that the food be dramatically, attractively, and appetizingly served. It was

It was not enough that the food tasted good. It was to be brought to the table triumphantly, almost theatrically.

not enough that the food tasted good; it was to be brought to the table triumphantly, almost theatrically.

During the last six months of Pani's ownership of the Colony, he employed a manager named M. Achille Borgo. In Borgo there was more courtesy, *savoir-faire,* and resourcefulness than one would have found in the ceremony master of a Hapsburg king.

For instance, on December 31, 1921, the telephone rang in the lobby of the Colony. My father and Borgo, who had been staring disconsolately at the depressing list of reservations for New Year's Eve, leaped for the phone. Borgo got there first. The woman caller on the other end turned out to be one of the great ladies of New York society. She had decided to forego New Year's Eve at the Plaza if Borgo could assure her that a ripsnorting party would be in progress at the Colony. He assured her that yes indeed there was going to be a large crowd, that the evening would be amusing, and that the atmosphere would be utterly hilarious. He then said he would TRY to reserve a good table for her.

Immediately after the call, Borgo phoned a dozen or so persons to invite them to the Colony for the evening. However, when the *grande dame* arrived with her six guests, they had the entire place to themselves. Except for a few lonely souls, the place was as dead as a tomb. Borgo couldn't even bring in a crowd gratis. That evening he kept completely out of sight. He didn't have the courage to face the woman and her party.

The lady, who turned out to have a sense of humor, came in several days later for lunch. Sheepishly Borgo greeted her. She glanced at the empty room and then said, "Of course, I should have telephoned for a reservation."

"I must beg your pardon, Madame," apologized Borgo, "and to prove my repentance, allow me to send to your table a bottle of Roederer Brut, 1902, on the house."

The intelligent grace of this gesture was typical of the methods it was necessary to practice in those days. And it was my father, Hartmann, and Borgo who garnered the loyalty of the few customers, not Joe Pani. As time wore on, dad and Hartmann were in close touch with Ernest Cerutti. They often met on the sly and discussed the Colony. Their dream was, of course, to one day buy the place and turn it

*Borgo couldn't even bring in a crowd gratis. That evening he kept
completely out of sight.*

into a first-class restaurant. Pani was in the market for
selling, but the triumvirate knew he would never sell to his
own employees.

The price was twenty-five thousand dollars. Dad,
Ernest, and Hartmann were determined to buy, regardless
of how high the price. Knowing that Pani would be disin-
clined to sell to them, dad went to Sylvester Haberman, the
landlord, and explained their predicament. He asked Haberman to act as purchaser for them. Evidently the idea of three
enterprising young men owning the little restaurant in

his house appealed to Haberman and he consented. The trio rounded up the money—six thousand dollars apiece—and, together with a note for the remaining seven thousand dollars, handed it to Haberman. He in turn delivered the money to Pani along with his personal note for seven thousand dollars, to preserve the anonymity of the buyers. The deal was closed. Dad, Cerutti, and Hartmann owned the Colony Restaurant.

Triumphantly, the three celebrated their realized dream and formed their plans with toast after toast at a Third Avenue bar. The whole place would have to be redecorated, of course. Everything would have to be cleaned, curtains hung, rugs laid, kitchen modernized, staff increased. In ten days, the old Colony was the new Colony.

The second opening took place in March of 1922. What Joe Pani's thoughts were that evening are not known, but from that time on he was more or less out of the picture. As time went by he reconciled his relationship with the trio, for as business improved, Pani's stock of excellent pre-World War I wine and liquor—hidden in the caves of the Woodmanston Inn—found a market in the clientele of the Colony.

That evening, Cerutti and dad were on the spot in the lobby, suave and impeccable. Borgo was gone, for his brother, who owned two successful restaurants in Paris, had called him back to the City of Light. Hartmann was excelling in the kitchen. The trio, needless to say, were in a state of absolute euphoria. But when the evening was over and the till had been counted, their enthusiasm dimmed. The profit amounted to little more than one hundred dollars.

For the next three months, the Colony continued to face hard times. The gentlemen around town with secret mistresses shunned the place, for during the renovation they had found other suitable rendezvous. Things didn't look good. The three owners, along with the headwaiters, captains, waiters, chefs, salad men, vegetable girls, dishwashers, *dame de lavabo,* and the men's-room attendant, all prayed devoutly to St. Teodato, the patron saint of restaurants.

Despite the fact that by this time they all feared the worst, they worked devotedly, oblivious of the probable debacle. Hartmann literally never left the kitchen during that period, except for catnaps at night on one of the banquettes in the dining room. He rose at the crack of dawn to dispatch his help to markets, butchers and fisheries and to calculate as many tasks as a hundred housewives. Dad and Cerutti bustled around the kitchen and the restaurant with gusto, but the Colony still didn't catch on.

And then one night it happened. The reputation of the food finally superseded the reputation of the bistro. Dad went around to the tables of several elderly men and their protégées, and with enthusiasm told them in a whisper that Mrs. William K. Vanderbilt was sitting in the restaurant at that very moment with another lady!

"Absurd!" quipped the gentlemen. "What on earth would a great lady like Mrs. Vanderbilt be doing in a place like the Colony?" Skeptical glances swept the room. Yes, it was Mrs. William K. Vanderbilt!

Overnight it happened. That evening Mrs. Vanderbilt was a customer at the Colony. The next evening, in came Joe Widener, the racing-horse and stable owner. Reginald Vanderbilt followed. The McCormicks appeared. Finally State Senator James J. Walker, the future mayor of New York City, entered. All were impressed with the Colony's food, atmosphere and service, and with the personalities of its owners.

The following night, William K. Vanderbilt himself came in. An arch gourmet, Vanderbilt had decided to try the place on the recommendation of his wife. He consistently dined out and found it difficult to discover a place that he could "repeat." After his first visit, William K.

The next evening, in came Joe Widener, the racing-horse and stable owner.

Vanderbilt was a regular until his death. To the surprise of dad and his then-partner, George Fiorentino, he left them two thousand dollars apiece.

The wealthy playboys around town who had formerly brought their mistresses to the Colony were now bringing their wives, who had heard about the place and insisted on dining there. In just three short months, the raffish Colony became the *raffiné* Colony, "the" place to lunch or sup.

During that period, Reginald Vanderbilt put the final seal of approval on the Colony by bringing his sixteen-year-old daughter there for the superb homemade ice cream. The young Miss Vanderbilt took to the ice cream like a hippie to pot, and soon began to invite her school chums for ice cream at the Colony. On one occasion she brought a dear classmate, a Miss Morgan, to dine with her father. Reginald Vanderbilt married her, and their daughter, Gloria Vanderbilt, is today Mrs. Wyatt Cooper.

In a short time, the till grew from one hundred dollars a day profit to one thousand. In the short span of three months the Colony was transformed from a rendezvous for illicit lovers into the second home of New York's first families.

And what exactly, initially, was the secret of its success? Luck only? Certainly not. The proprietors' charm, a good location, cozy atmosphere, ready charge accounts were all factors, but primarily the Colony featured something hitherto unknown in the city. That was the unusual. Where else could you order durian, a luscious Malayan fruit, and have it brought to the table without the blink of an eye from the waiter? Where else could you get a melon that had been nourished with brandy while ripening? Where else would a restaurant pay sixty dollars for a crate of asparagus? Only at the Colony. Yes, in those days $2.50 was a lot of money to pay for a plate of asparagus. But it was the very first and the very best season, and for that people paid.

Where else could you get the best liquor during Prohibition? Only at the Colony. In those days the liquor was kept in an elevator at 667 Madison Avenue. When the doorman gave the signal that the Feds were approaching, the chief barman, Marco Hattem, simply ran the elevator up to the top floor.

Of course there were times when the Federal agents were on the premises dining. One evening two agents were there and inquired what was being served in the demitasse cups at the next table. Dad immediately answered, "Brandy, but not the horrible stuff you are used to confiscating!" The agents were so taken with his straightforward charm, as well as some of the excellent brandy, that they swore eternal secrecy and friendship.

During the first year, the Colony cleared seventy-five thousand dollars. But that was only the beginning. The twenties were days of quick and easy money and the income climbed steadily.

People ate, people spent, and the triumvirate reportedly cleared half a million dollars during the heyday of the Roaring Twenties.

In 1926 the entrance to the Colony was moved from 667 Madison Avenue to around the corner on 61st Street. The eccentric Dr. Burke had passed on, and his office was appropriated to enlarge the bar. Air conditioning was installed, a Colony first for New York. The biggest names in this hemisphere—and the other half of the world—congregated there. If you were to drop in any day, you could expect to see the King of Greece, Charlie Chaplin, a few Astors and Vanderbilts, Gloria Swanson, Bernard Baruch, the Prince of Wales, Connie Bennett, the Churchills, Wallace Warfield, the Crown Prince of Sweden, George S. Kaufman, Eleanor Roosevelt, Otto Kahn, Queen Zita, Jules S. Bache, Lords Northcliff and Rothmere, the Duc de Guise, Louis B. Mayer, Prince Youssupoff, the King of Siam, Preston Sturges, Archduke Otto, Helen Hayes, Lord Beaverbrook, Alexander Korda, and on and on and on. During that period the Colony already had over two thousand charge accounts.

Soon, columnists began to frequent the Colony and to report daily the comings and goings of the restaurant's guests.

During the stock-market crash of 1929 and the Depression that followed, the Colony suffered along with everyone else. Many of the former customers stayed away. Others continued to come in, even though they didn't have the cash to pay the bill. The owners sympathized and didn't press for payment, allowing great amounts of credit. Many people who had been good customers were fed on the house. There were also total strangers who came in without a *sou*. Case in point, a young man who had consumed a large, well-selected dinner in the company of two young ladies came out to the lobby and approached dad. He bowed politely and inquired, "Yes, sir, what can I do for you?"

"I'm afraid you don't know me, Mr. Cavallero," said the somewhat down-and-out and yet distinguished-looking lad, "but I must tell you that I can't pay for the dinner. I don't have a cent."

Dad's eyes widened and he said, "Come up to my office."

Once there, he reached into the strongbox and handed a hundred-dollar bill to the young man. "You need a new suit. Better buy one. And until you get on your feet, you may eat here free. But don't you think one woman is sufficient for a man down on his luck?"

The young fellow took dad's advice. He left the ladies home and dined at the Colony for a long time. The owner's "headwaiter instinct" proved accurate. In the years that followed, the man went on to become one of the top directors in motion pictures. When in New York, he virtually lived at the Colony.

As the years passed, the triumvirate slowly dissolved. In 1927 Hartmann sold his share to dad and Ernest and traveled back to Alsace. Then in 1937 Cerutti sold his share to dad. On the way back to his native Italy, Cerutti died suddenly on board an Italian liner. The great restaurateur left an estate of nearly half a million dollars. In 1939 George Fiorentino, who had been headwaiter since the early days of the Colony, joined dad as a partner.

As I look back over my association with the Colony, I recall the first time my father gave me the grand tour of the restaurant. I was twelve years old and remember being very impressed with the large pots in the kitchen. That seems to be the only thing I remember. I also recall, after one year at Fordham University, my short stay at the Hotel Management School at Cornell. Every time the professor attempted to explain in class how this or that was done, I always raised my hand and said, "That's good in theory but actually it's done this way." I only lasted four months in the course due to insubordination. Actually, most successful restaurant men are brought up in the business. You cannot learn in college what nitty-gritty experience can teach. A course in restaurant management is valuable to a person who has not been brought up in the business, as a student will learn all about bookkeeping, food and beverage control, and accounting. However, it simply cannot teach you how to run a restaurant.

While attending Fordham I worked part-time in the kitchen of the Biltmore Hotel, and after that—in order to improve my knowledge of foreign languages, as well as of restaurant operation—my father sent me off to Europe to work in several hotels. My first job abroad was in Paris at the George V Hotel. My father sent me to Mr. Blouet. "Here he is," he said. "Do with him what you can." When I arrived, Mr. Blouet asked me if I could speak French. When I replied that I did speak a little French, I was promptly

placed at the switchboard. The confusion became unbear-
able and after a short while I was demoted to the kitchen to
wash dishes. Within two weeks, in self-defense, I did master
French well enough to get out of the kitchen and into the
dining room. I also served at the reception desk.

My European experience taught me to respect the
hierarchy of restaurant employees from top to bottom. As I
watched, I learned that a waiter in a first-class restaurant
must know what to bring to the table with what, he must
know how long the preparation of the food takes and how it
is to be served, he must be able to coordinate five or six
tables with the forty or fifty separate items that must be
served, all complicated and different. The job requires a
great deal of experience and know-how. An experienced,
professional waiter must also be something of an artist.

Following my European training, I assisted my father
in the management of the Colony for ten years before I
became a partner in the business.

During those early years, I learned that "the best of
the first of a season" became a rule at the Colony. Three or
four weeks before anyone else was serving asparagus, the
Colony had it on the menu. A case of the king of vegetables
can cost as much as sixty or seventy dollars, but I never
quibbled. I may have lost money on the item, but from a
public-relations point of view we got a head start on our
competition.

White baits and soft-shell crab are other items that we
had on our menu before anyone else. When grouse season
opened in Scotland on August 12, grouse was on the Colony's table on the thirteenth.

In addition to the "best of the first," the Colony had
many firsts in the food and wine area. Broccoli was first
served, and served properly, at the Colony. Other restaurants that followed in the Colony's footsteps did serve it, but

since they didn't know how to prepare broccoli properly, it always appeared on the table as a mushy mess.

Dom Pérignon champagne was also first served in this country at the Colony. When the then Cardinal Pacelli paid a visit to the United States many years ago, a Mrs. Brady who was his hostess in the United States imported a case of Dom Pérignon from France. When the Cardinal came to the Colony for dinner, Mrs. Brady sent the case of fine wine to the restaurant. After the dinner was over, my father sampled the two or three bottles left. He thought it was the best wine he had ever tasted and immediately arranged with Moët and Chandon to import it. Pacelli, of course, went on to become Pope. This marked another first for the Colony as the only restaurant in the United States to have ever had a future or present Pope for dinner.

About thirty years ago another first occurred at the Colony. Lionel, Lord Tennyson, grandson of the poet, excused himself after dinner and adjourned to the men's room. He seemed horrified as he returned to the table. On his way back he met my father and turned to him reproachfully, "What, Gene! You have no bidets in your men's room? How can you operate a decent place without them?" Dad always took the whims of his customers seriously. "No, my lord," he said, "I haven't got them. But since your lordship has brought them to my attention, they'll be put in tomorrow."

The following day bidets were installed in both the men's and ladies' rooms. The ladies were appalled. "What do you think we are?" they exclaimed. "French hussies?" "We do bathe twice a day, you know." Dad had the bidet removed from the ladies' room, but the one in the men's room stayed put for several years, until a plethora of practical jokes forced removal. The two bidets were eventually bought by a Paris-minded couple who installed them in one of the bathrooms of their Virginia country house.

Through the years a great number of stories have come out of the Colony. This is true of the history of any great restaurant and the Colony's is no exception. Along with the ubiquitous crises come the inevitable comedies. One of the most hair-raising incidents on the record occurred a number of years ago and concerned a fortune in jewels on display in the Van Cleef and Arpels vitrine in the lobby.

One Friday evening, at the height of the social season, one of New York's more sprightly young heifers was dining at the Colony. As she lingered over her *mousse au chocolat,* the gleam of the priceless gems in the lobby caught her eye. "Of course," she thought, "that's what I'll wear to the ball tonight!" She approached my father, Gene senior, and asked him if she might borrow them to wear to the charity gala she planned to attend later that evening. Obviously taken by her spirit, he said, "Certainly we'll loan them to you. Just return them tomorrow." He went to the jewel case and told the girl to take whatever she wanted. She selected an emerald necklace, diamond earrings, and a diamond-and-emerald bracelet, put them on, and breezed off into the night.

The jewels were not returned the following day. My father assumed that the young lady had kicked up her heels in excess and was "at home" resting. Surely she would show up for dinner that evening with the jewels. However, she did not.

"What to do?" he pondered. To telephone the girl was simply out of the question, as he certainly did not wish to imply in any way that something fishy had occurred. Instead, he telephoned the owner of the jewels and explained the situation. The man, who knew the young girl, was delighted that she had borrowed them and said, "They circulate, and it does them good to be worn, particularly by such a lovely creature. At any rate, don't worry, because they are insured for the full amount."

"Surely she will return them on Sunday," he thought.

Again she did not. On Monday, near-hysteria hit the Colony. The jewels had not yet been returned. My father finally decided that he would have to telephone and inquire about the missing jewels. The operator reported that the lady was not in. Furthermore, she had left town.

He decided to wait until Wednesday before taking more serious action. Despite the young lady's occasional forays into piquant adventure, she had an excellent reputation. It seemed impossible that she was up to tricks. In the meantime, his imagination ran wild. Had she been the victim of a holdup? Had she been kidnapped? Did she have amnesia? The entire mystery, of course, was kept strictly under wraps, as dad didn't wish the Colony to become involved in any kind of unsavory publicity or scandal.

Tuesday came and went. No jewels. Wednesday came. Still no jewels. Finally, around eight o'clock in the evening, he was approached in the lobby by a pretty black girl. She explained that she was the lady's maid, and handed him a little paper bag. He opened the bag, breathed a deep sigh of relief, and placed the missing jewels back in the vitrine.

Several days later the young lady herself came into the restaurant for dinner. My father approached her and said, "You know, we were somewhat concerned about the jewels you borrowed on Friday night." She apologized and offered the following explanation.

That Friday night after the ball, in her rush to leave town for the country, she had carelessly left the jewels on her vanity. The maid, who had been invited to a series of parties in Harlem over the weekend, thought they were some of Woolworth's best, picked them up, and wore them all weekend. When the girl had returned to town on Wednesday she noticed the jewels on her vanity and asked the maid to return them. "Why, they all thought it was junk jewelry!" quipped the maid. Little did they know that the jewels were worth well over $150,000.

A man asked the captain for a menu, and then escaped with $100,000 in Van Cleef and Arpels jewels from the vitrine.

The same Van Cleef and Arpels vitrine was, however, the object of the most sensational robbery ever to occur at the Colony. Several years ago, at around four in the afternoon, a man came into the restaurant and asked the captain if he could see the menu for the evening. The captain went to get the menu. By the time he had returned, the vitrine had been opened and emptied of its contents, worth over one hundred thousand dollars. The thief escaped and the jewels were never recovered.

Petty pilferage is par for the course in any great restaurant, and is often the source of great hilarity. It can truly be said that almost anything that is not nailed to the floor is marked "up for grabs" by clever souvenir hunters and pranksters. The classic Colony story concerns an elegant New York hostess who had asked me to cater a party at her home. I arrived at the beautifully appointed apartment and, upon starting the direction of the preparation of the dinner, inquired of the lady of the house if she had any pepper mills. "Oh," she said, "yes, I have plenty." She didn't, however, tell me where they were. As the tables were set, and time drew near for the arrival of the first guests, I again inquired as to the location of the mills. "Look in the right-hand cabinet in the kitchen," the lady then said. "There are dozens of them in there."

I looked and discovered over two dozen pepper mills. I mused for a while over this plethora of simple machinery. At the same time, it occurred to me that they resembled those in use at the Colony. Upon looking inside the mills, I found the Colony seal in each and every one. Rather than mention it to the lady, I simply placed three of them on the tables set for dinner. Then, at the end of the evening, I stole all of them back from the hostess. Needless to say, the incident has never been mentioned by the lady.

There are times when petty theft must be handled with tact and humor. One such incident occurred a few years ago when a rather sprightly lady was seen placing her mink coat on the table for a moment as she rose from her dinner. One of the waiters noted that a wine bucket was under the coat and flagged me.

When she hurriedly made her way into the lobby and out the door, we knew what was going on but we all sat tight. Presuming it was a joke, we didn't wish to spoil her fun. After she got outside, she turned on her heels and came back into the restaurant, explained that the prank was performed on a dare, and proclaimed her triumph by returning the bucket and collecting a hundred dollars from her party.

When it comes to handling a crisis, there is a quality that appears to be inherent in most successful restaurateurs. It is called the "headwaiter's instinct." It is perhaps best illustrated by an incident that occurred several years ago. A gentleman known about town as a free spender had been a good customer at the Colony for years. Then one day he had a sudden and debilitating financial reverse. This, however, did not keep him away from the Colony. He came in and spoke to me, explaining that although he couldn't really afford the prices, he would like to come in once in a while and entertain his friends. "Someday, I will pay you back," he said. I thought for a while and then agreed that it would be all right. For several months the man continued to come in for dinner, eating moderately but nonetheless running up a bill of over two thousand dollars. My father reprimanded me severely for extending such unlimited credit.

Nonetheless, I stuck to my guns and insisted that the risk was a good one. Then suddenly the man disappeared. He had left town and nobody knew where he had gone. I surmised that perhaps my judgment had been in error, but still held high hopes of one day receiving payment for the bill.

Almost a year later, at Christmas time, an elegant leather wallet arrived in the mail. It contained a check for the two thousand dollars, plus another three thousand dollars to "keep as credit in the event that I should ever run out of money again and wish to dine in your restaurant." The money is being held for the man, although he has never to this day shown up to dine on his credit. He now lives somewhere in the Middle East, and according to all reports has once again struck it rich. Apparently he was so very disappointed in his friends and business colleagues when he hit bad times that he has never wished to return to New York.

Occasionally, unpleasant situations arose as a result of checkroom swindling. Unfortunately, there are people in this world who will take advantage of the grace, manners, and dignity of a fine old institution for their own financial gain. Several years ago a lady who now and then dined at the Colony came in for lunch. Upon leaving, she claimed that she had left a suitcase full of clothes in the checkroom. I searched high and low and could not find the missing

A lady claimed a misplaced suitcase had $4000 worth of clothes in it.

valise anywhere. I asked her, "Are you absolutely positive that you brought it in with you?"

"Of course I am," she answered, "and further, it had four thousand dollars' worth of clothes in it." She followed this statement by a threat to sue if the suitcase didn't show up.

I called my attorney, who told me to hold off for a few days, for the missing bag might turn up somewhere. Sure enough, three days later a cabbie, saying that a fare had left it in his taxi before entering the restaurant, deposited a suitcase at the Colony that matched the description given by the lady who had threatened to sue. The next day the bag was opened in the lady's presence, revealing a collection of cheap bargain-basement clothing worth at most fifty dollars. The lady settled for the return of her bag and has never since entered the Colony.

One evening the scene at the checkroom almost caused my blood to run cold, for as I glanced around I caught sight of a man taking a revolver out of his pocket. I walked over to the man and he said, "You own this place, don't you?"

"Yes, I do," I replied.

The customer handed me the gun. "Here, take care of this until after dinner," he requested.

I took it up to my office and placed it in my safe. When the man finished his dinner, he retrieved his revolver and quietly left the restaurant.

On another occasion a customer from out of town came into the checkroom and asked to leave twenty-five thousand dollars in cash and jewelry "until I come back next week."

The incident of the ermine coat goes down as the "real-money" story in the annals of the Colony. One evening, after all of the customers had departed, I noticed a white ermine coat hanging in the checkroom. Whoever owned it had forgotten to claim it. It was put away in the safe after having been valued at twenty-five thousand dollars. Two months later, a lady called and asked, "Did I leave my white coat at your restaurant?" A month after that she came in to claim it.

Naturally, people do leave things behind in restaurants, and the Colony collected more than its share of handbags, boots, umbrellas, and raincoats. At least a hundred pairs of eyeglasses were left each year. These were donated to "New Eyes for the Needy" in Short Hills, New Jersey.

Jewels have been left behind in the ladies' room but are generally retrieved within a day or two. One time, however, a very large diamond remained in the safe for three months before it was claimed.

Among the more unlikely things left behind was a set of false teeth. After the dishes leave the table, they are taken to the kitchen, where they are scraped. One of the hands in the kitchen discovered the false teeth on a plate. The man who owned them had left the restaurant and was in a taxi before he realized that he had lost his teeth. He did return to claim them.

One evening a busboy called dad over to a table to see a most bizarre sight. Next to an empty champagne glass was a glass eye! The lady who owned it evidently had changed the color of her synthetic eye right there at the table. The glass eye was never reclaimed.

Occasionally, accents and language barriers create amusing incidents, testifying to the international tenor of the help as well as of the clientele. One evening, for example, I noticed a rather animated waiter taking a dessert order from a customer. All appeared to be in order, except that the waiter seemed to be questioning the customer again and again about the dessert. Five minutes passed, and I noticed that the dessert had not yet arrived at the table. "What about the dessert at Table 20? Is it on its way?" I inquired of the waiter.

The waiter looked skeptically at me and replied, "Yes, yes, it's coming."

Five minutes more passed and still the dessert had not arrived. I went to the captain and proceeded to reprimand him. "Why isn't the dessert on the table?" I demanded. The captain went to the waiter and a very animated conversation ensued between the two. I passed by again and this time said, "I'm coming back here in two minutes and expect to see the dessert on the table."

Finally the dessert arrived. The waiter took a pitcher of sweet cream and to the wide-eyed amazement of the customer poured it over the dessert. I rushed to the table, and there in front of the diner was a plateful of rubber bands

*The waiter took a pitcher of sweet cream and to the wide-eyed
amazement of the customer poured it over the dessert. I rushed to the
table, and there in front of the diner was a plateful of rubber bands
covered with cream!*

covered with cream! "The gentleman insisted on having
them, so I brought them," the waiter explained. It turned
out that the man had ordered rhubarb, and that the waiter
had mistaken the word for rubber bands.

Another evening, a woman on the brink of giving birth
came in for dinner. She planned on going to the hospital
immediately after dinner. However, upon finishing her meal
and ordering a Drambuie, she suddenly went into labor. She
claimed it was merely cramps, but I knew better. "No babies
born in the dining room," is an unwritten rule at the
Colony. I quickly cased the restaurant for a doctor and, yes,
there was a doctor in the house. He informed the expectant
mother that she had less than one hour to get to a hospital,
took her there in his own car, and then returned to finish his
dinner.

Colony rule: No babies born in the dining room.

CHAPTER TWO

An Inside Look and
a Little Bit of Advice

Everyone dines out on occasion, but very few people really understand what they can do to assure themselves a pleasant dining experience. In the first place, why go out to dine at all?

True, different people go out for different reasons. First there are those who wish to be seen, then those who wish to see, those who go to be entertained, and finally, those who go out to eat good food.

After many years. I've concluded that there is no better place to entertain than in a restaurant. When a host invites eight or ten people to his home for dinner, he begins to worry. First he wonders whether his cook, his wife, or he himself will be able to prepare the food properly. Then he is concerned about whether his guests will like the food. Will the waitress or butler serve it properly? Does he have the right wines? Naturally, a host wants to please his guests or he wouldn't have invited them in the first place.

In a restaurant, a host can relax and be concerned solely with entertaining his guests. The waiters will provide better service than his maid at home. A kitchen manned by fifteen or twenty people and a staff of expert chefs is far better able to prepare dinner than an "at-home" kitchen and cook. Further, the kitchen in a restaurant can turn out the most complicated and lavish or the simplest and most delicious food imaginable. A host cannot do this in his own home. He doesn't have the equipment. He must plan days or weeks in advance. In short, entertaining six or eight people for dinner in a restaurant will be a pleasure for the host as well as for his guests. One need only reserve the table, order a lovely dinner, and let the management worry about seeing that all goes well. Furthermore, there is no mess to clean up afterward. And if something should go wrong, the management and staff are there to correct it.

There is one thing you might keep in mind when entertaining in a restaurant. If you have invited eight people for dinner, ordinarily these people will be ordering eight different soups, eight different entrées, eight different vegetables, eight different salads, and eight different desserts. To assure that everything goes well, why not place your order with the restaurant several days in advance? If guests come to your home, you serve one or two different dishes to them. Why not do the same in a restaurant? By so doing, you will avoid long waits between courses and everyone will have a

Will the waitress or butler serve it properly?

much more pleasant time. It's only common sense to realize that it often takes an hour to cook one entrée and fifteen minutes for another. An entire table will be kept waiting for the serving of the food. In order to avoid confusion, and out of consideration for your guests, order dinner for them. Should one of your guests prefer something else, you can always change that person's order.

Personally, I don't enjoy eating at home with my wife and family. My wife is a superb cook, and my children are all gourmets—much more so than I am, in fact. But when I'm home on a Sunday, my wife goes into the kitchen at four o'clock and emerges at seven. She prepares a superb six-course gourmet dinner, and then spends another few hours cleaning up the mess. This is not pleasant to me, for I don't even see her, and after the meal is over, she's dog-tired.

In a restaurant, I have the opportunity to enjoy her when she is at her best. She's not concerned about when this or that will be ready or about cleaning up afterward. The entire meal is a pleasure. In addition, I can order what I wish to eat and don't have to eat what is set before me. Furthermore, my idea of a civilized meal is to sit for four hours over dinner. This is unfair to my wife at home. No meal is worth four hours of preparation, four hours of dining, and two hours of cleaning up.

When you dine out, there are many things that you should remember. First of all, any restaurant worth its salt wishes to please you and to provide a pleasant dining experience. The waiters, captains, wine stewards, managers are all there to help you enjoy yourself. Don't hesitate to call on them for help or advice.

For instance, ask the wine steward about wines. If you don't know your wine, you can rely upon him to order something within reason that will complement your meal. A good restaurant will never try to sell you an expensive bottle of wine; they don't want you to feel that you're being taken. At the Colony a moderately priced good wine was generally recommended. It pays to take this advice, for if you are dining in a good restaurant, the staff will not bring you something inferior or something too expensive. They wish to please you. It is common sense to take their recommendations.

The general public believes that the items on the menu are the only things served in a restaurant. In a first-class restaurant, menus are used only for suggestions. If the menu listed everything available in the restaurant, it would read like a Bible. The menu is but a suggestion sheet. Look at it, perhaps decide to have something that is listed, or maybe a listing on the menu will inspire you to order a dish that you may have had there or elsewhere in the past.

In ordering, many customers will peruse the menu and, because it is written in French, will order steak. If you don't understand the menu, or if you don't recognize the dish mentioned, never be afraid to ask the captain to explain it to you. That is one of his primary responsibilities. He's there to help you enjoy a good dinner and will translate and explain how the dishes are prepared. It only stands to reason that you, the diner, couldn't possibly understand every item on the menu and the way it is prepared.

Many restaurants offer a *plat du jour*. A lot of customers will shy away from ordering this specially prepared dish because they feel that it must be something left over from the day before that the restaurant wishes to unload. In any fine restaurant, the reverse is true. The *plat du jour* is specially prepared in many cases, a great treat that may have taken days to prepare. If a waiter recommends the dish, don't be a doubting Thomas. Take his word for it. Any restaurant worth its salt will never try to stick you with something inferior.

Wine and spirits comprise a category dear to the hearts of all who enjoy dining in the grand manner. Unfortunately, American drinking habits are not particularly conducive to enjoyable dining. How can anyone even taste food after having had three or four martinis before dinner? Two drinks before dinner are enough. Have the cocktails, then sit down and enjoy dining with a glass of wine. If serious drinking is what you have in mind, please wait until after dinner.

As for ordering wine in a restaurant, here again most patrons are confused, and with good reason. The wine merchants have created such an aura of mystery around vintages, names, and sources that many people are afraid to order. You should experiment and find out what you enjoy. Moderately priced American or French wines abound, and you will undoubtedly find one that is to your taste. In addition, stick to the seven- or eight-dollar wines. Twenty dollars for a bottle of wine is too much money unless you are really a connoisseur. If you like red wine, drink

Two drinks before dinner are enough.

---

it; if you like white, drink that. Don't fall for the red-with-meat, white-with-fish line. That is personal taste. The *sommelier* is there to assist you in your selection. You can always count on his recommendations in a fine restaurant.

Just a short word on brandy. It is the drink of geniuses. The reason is that it does put the body to sleep, but the mind will continue to work while you sleep. This is not true of other spirits.

The wine expert is a laugh. Consider how many times you have heard pretentious prattle about what side of what mountain in which district a certain wine comes from. Or that the sun in 1959 on this or that side of this or that mountain was responsible for the wine's excellence. Or that the boat ran into rough water in the North Atlantic three days out. Anyone can tell a good wine from a bad wine, just as a ten-year-old boy knows a good oyster from a bad oyster.

Because many people are unsure of whether to order red or white wine, rosé has become enormously popular. I feel that most rosé wine is terrible. It is neither red nor white, and in most cases is manufactured. Some rosé wines are not manufactured, but they are rare.

As for wine cellars, I feel that they too are pretentious. At home, I keep two bottles of Souave and two of Nuits-Saint-Georges. Why buy expensive wines that spoil easily when so many wines are available that do not spoil? And further, to have a proper wine cellar, the temperature, humidity, and light must be perfect. It is senseless to buy expensive wines to store, only to have them ruined by improper conditions.

One last word on wines and spirits, and, unfortunately, a necessary one. Occasionally a woman came into the Colony and ordered whiskey in a shot glass. There is nothing more appalling than seeing a woman swilling down whiskey from a shot glass. The double shot is another horrendous social error. If two shots is what a woman wants, by all means serve them, but one shot at a time. At the Colony we served a single shot in a brandy glass and a double shot in a big brandy glass. Finally, in the same category—despite the fact that the ladies have indeed come a long way—there is still nothing more disagreeable, unreasonable, and unladylike than a female lush.

There are first-class restaurants that have a bad name insofar as tipping to get a table. This is a carry-over from the

Women who drink too much . . .

days of World War II, when help was short and five dollars did the trick with the headwaiter. Today, if there is a table available, most headwaiters will give it to you with pleasure.

Many people who are good tippers feel that they have the right to be disagreeable. A large tip never guarantees good service. Waiters work hard at serving people who they know aren't going to tip a large amount. However, they know that these people appreciate everything done for them, so they go ahead and work like the devil. They will even work harder for people who are appreciative and understand their problems than for the fellow who raises hell and gives a fifty-dollar tip.

I would like to turn now to the subject of the operation of a successful restaurant. First of all, it is a fantastically complex and expensive operation. With expenses the way they are these days, a restaurant has to be very successful and the owners very clever in order to eke out a reasonable profit on the investment. Bear in mind that it takes many years before a restaurant really begins to make a profit. If, for example, there are six months of good business, three weeks of bad business can wipe out the profit.

Just maintaining a clean and freshly decorated place can amount to great sums of money. We spent close to fifty thousand dollars a year just on maintenance! This consisted of cleaning carpets, putting up fresh draperies, cleaning and reinsulating refrigerators, hanging doors, ripping apart and overhauling ovens, shampooing and cleaning upholstery, repairing broken chairs and tables. We continuously cleaned and repaired everything in the restaurant.

It was important that we spend this money, because a restaurant should never look dog-eared and shopworn. It can be chic in the décor of past eras, but it should always be fresh, clean, and crisp. Many restaurants find they're going downhill after four or five years. Shabbiness is a contributing factor in these cases. The owners may think that people don't notice it, but customers get the feeling that the place is going to seed and stop coming in.

Another thing the public doesn't seem to realize is that the restaurant business suffers a great deal during bad weather. When it rains or snows, transportation is hard to come by. Cabs are a problem and you can't get a limo. New York is the only city in the world where people stay home

because they hear over the radio that there is to be a thunder-
storm. If it gets too cold or too warm early in the season, our
business is affected. The ladies aren't prepared. Their fur
coats are in the cleaner's or their spring suits are too warm
for the hot weather. The ladies prefer to stay home until
they can dress properly. A new restaurant will suffer financial reverses from one hot spring or one chilly autumn.

Any successful restaurant owes its success not only to
its management but to its personnel. If the staff take a
personal interest in the restaurant, they can contribute more
to the success of a place than you can imagine. When the
chips are down, they perform fantastic feats that can't be
understood by people not in the business. When the transport strike occurred, for instance, my waiters and help got
here on their own initiative. During the blackout, the help
was magnificent. In fact, it was one of our best nights.

A successful restaurant must also be versatile. We have
a French kitchen, but prepare some German and Italian
dishes better than they do in Germany and Italy. In our
kitchen we have French, German, and Spanish chefs. Our
waiters are Italian. The international kitchen has made the
restaurant something other than solely French. It is international in the true sense of the word.

Another quality that makes for an interesting, amusing,
and successful restaurant is a mixed clientele. At the Colony,
our customers included dancers, socialites, business people,
street cleaners, executives, royalty, and diplomats. That was
one of our secrets. To cater to any one group of people
marks your doom. Suddenly the restaurant becomes one
big club, and people get tired of looking at the same old
faces. Customers like to see movie stars, artists, bankers,
lawyers, gamblers, and even members of the Mafia. We
never judged the morality of our customers. It was our business to serve our patrons to the best of our ability. Placing
an actress at a table next to a socialite led to an interesting

Some of our customers desired privacy. They wished to be somewhere where they wouldn't be annoyed.

evening for both. On the other hand, some of our customers desired privacy. They wished to be somewhere where people wouldn't annoy them. An autograph request was all right with us, but any other infringement on the privacy of our customers was not permitted at the Colony.

Ignoring customers unknown to the restaurant is a serious mistake many restaurateurs make. At the Colony, a stranger was accorded more attention than a steady customer. We felt that the steady customer was already our devotee. We had him hooked, but we had to constantly build up our clientele. The way to do this is to take exceptional care of a newcomer. He then becomes a good customer, and that, of course, is good for business.

Turning now to the restaurant man himself, most people think of him as a glamorous individual. He greets his customers, calls celebrities by name and wines and dines them. However, he is also a plumber, psychiatrist, marriage counselor, referee, bouncer, electrician, accountant, lawyer, dishwasher, friend, servant—in short, a jack of all trades. He also works close to eighteen hours a day. Restaurant men rarely see their wives. It isn't because they don't love them, mind you, but they are also married to their business. Restaurant men's wives must be the most understanding women in the world.

Furthermore, a restaurant owner must be like the coach of a football team. All facets of the business must be coordinated, and the restaurant man is responsible for this. If the food is not properly prepared in the kitchen, the waiter can't serve it. If the food is properly prepared and the waiter doesn't bring it out at the proper moment, the entire meal can be spoiled. A captain taking an order and transmitting it improperly to a waiter can ruin a dinner. The restaurant man must keep an eagle eye on every phase of his business at all times.

Restaurant men who have been brought up in the business will rarely if ever criticize another restaurateur. Theirs is a very closed and loyal fraternity. And no restaurant man likes to hear his customer complain about another restaurant he has frequented. When this happened to me, I tried to explain to my customer that mistakes do happen once in a while. Perhaps the chef was ill or tables had to be shifted at the last minute. Often the restaurant was owned by a good friend of mine and I didn't like to hear such criticism.

Finally, believe it or not, restaurant men do react to the public. Most people don't understand what the restaurant business is and what the restaurateur's point of view is. To the restaurant man, not all the public is wonderful and always right, just as not all restaurants are wonderful.

Indeed, there were customers who did understand what we were trying to do. There were times when we made ghastly mistakes and were courteously and understandingly forgiven. Our list of civilized, gracious, and grateful ladies and gentlemen would fill an entire chapter of this book and the stories of true kindness another.

There were times, however, when frankly you felt like punching a customer right smack in the nose. There was a customer who had been coming to the Colony for over twenty years. He always had the same captain. Six days a week he came in for lunch and two or three times a week for dinner. The captain had served his needs dutifully and devotedly for those twenty years. Then one day the captain dropped dead. The following day the customer came in. I had thought and thought about exactly how I would be able to tell him of the sad news. They had, after all, been friends for years. I finally went up to him and said, "I don't know how to tell you this, but Mr. X., your captain, dropped dead yesterday."

The customer looked me straight in the face and said, "Oh, really? Who's my captain today?"

CHAPTER THREE

And Opinions

Although a restaurateur's primary concern is to supervise the operation of his restaurant, he is in addition irrevocably and without choice drawn into the worlds of fashion, cookbooks, wines, food experts, and customer behavior.

In recalling my experiences as owner of the Colony, I could—to coin a phrase—write a book. Hence, and at the risk of raising some hackles, I venture some opinions.

Naturally, the Colony was frequently the stage for the display of the latest in fashion. And, although catering to

the whims of the *haute couture* has always been an integral
part of a smart restaurateur's operation, these days more
often than not it is a matter of tactful coping.

Unfortunately, the era of dressing for dinner has all but
vanished. Today men come into the restaurant in the evening dressed in blue or gray business suits. The excuse offered is that it is too much trouble to get into dinner clothes.
Truthfully, is it any more difficult to change into dinner
clothes than to change into a standard blue suit? The ladies,
of course, still turn out in beautiful clothes, but why can't
they prevail upon their husbands or escorts to change into
dinner clothes? Nothing looks nicer in a restaurant than a
dining room full of attractive people in evening clothes, and
what could be more chic?

At the Colony, if customers came in dressed in dinner
clothes, they were always given a good table. In fact, one of
the secrets of getting a good table or a table at all in a busy
restaurant is to dress in dinner clothes, as all restaurants like
to have elegantly dressed customers. And from the point of
view of the gentlemen, who doesn't feel better dressed in
dinner clothes and a crisp white shirt with studs?

One of my pet peeves are hats on women. Ninety per
cent of the ladies look ghastly in them. Milliners sell a bill
of goods to unsuspecting women, and then turn them out
onto the street looking like freaks. When I first got married,
I took all of my wife's hats and threw them out. And she
happened to be a John Frederics model! Some women do
look good in hats, but they are the exceptions. And these
women always wear the same style, perhaps in a different
color but the style that they have found is enormously
flattering to them.

In the past few years, the mini-skirt has presented a
ticklish situation. Where do decency and taste begin and
end? The line must be drawn somewhere, and that is something I decide myself. One evening a pretty young girl came

into the Colony and sat down in the lobby. I took one look at her, walked over and said, "I'd appreciate it very much if you would stand up while you wait for your escort."

"I don't know why you're upset," she very sharply replied. "After all, I am wearing panties."

I firmly told her to stand up and she did. Ten minutes later when her escort arrived, she complained bitterly about the incident. Her date grabbed her by the hand, angrily said, "Gene is right," and dragged her out of the restaurant.

Even more recently, the Paris-Seventh Avenue axis has exploded and revolted with some wildly imaginative if not particularly tasteful new concepts—the topless or peek-a-boo dress, for example. I felt that exposed breasts had no place in my restaurant. Not only does nudity offend or distract most of my customers, but it wreaks utter havoc with the help. Last year a women came into the Colony and removed her jacket, revealing a non-dress that was unquestionably out of order. I rushed to her table and insisted that she replace her jacket. In the meantime, two wide-eyed young waiters, recently arrived from Europe, dropped the china they had been holding in their trembling hands. The woman did replace her jacket, but not before sharply informing me that I was old-fashioned. It turned out that she was a notorious publicity hound around town and had worn the same costume to several other elegant restaurants.

The controversy surrounding the pants suit rather absurdly became the storm in the Colony's teacup. Pants on women may be "in," but to me they were still slacks and not particularly becoming to most women. Shortly after pants suits were first shown in Paris, a woman arrived at the Colony wearing one. She had just come in from the airport and had not had time to change her clothes. She asked if she might come in "just this once." I seated her, but when on the following day seven or eight women came in dressed in pants, I firmly turned them down.

The next day the papers were full of reports of the incident. Two more women came in dressed in pants suits. Again I refused them, and received a round of applause from a dozen ladies who were lunching in the dining room. Two of the ladies, in fact, came up to me and kissed me. Hundreds of letters poured in on the subject, and the fashion magazines mushroomed the incident into a *cause célèbre*. Fashion editors began arriving dressed in pants suits to see if they could get away with it. "Who would be the first?" became the talk of the fashion world. "When will Gene give in?" I finally did when I seated the ladies *if* they were wearing very nice pants suits. But while the ban was in effect I turned away ten ladies a day.

It used to be that male attire was fairly standard. A restaurateur had only to cope with tieless gentlemen. However, recently the standards of male dress have become increasingly complex. With the *couture* for men, new tactics have necessarily evolved. For instance, long-haired young men are always welcome, *if* the hair is cared for, neat, clean, and attractive. No one can object to that. However, when curls run down the back or the hair is dirty, objections are in order.

Mod clothes such as pink shirts with purple ties with yellow jackets and orange shoes are fine for the stage or for Third Avenue bars or discotheques, but they were definitely out of place at the Colony. In the same sense, a roomful of turtle-necked male diners without the beads or medallions would more resemble a truck drivers' convention than an elegant restaurant. Turtle necks were not permitted at the Colony.

Turning now to the subject of food experts and gourmets, I feel they fall into two categories—the professional and the amateur. Both are fakes. Most restaurant critics rate a restaurant on the basis of one visit. This is not only unfair, it is impossible. A restaurant must be visited at least three or four times before one even begins to get some idea of the caliber of the food. Often an expert will have ten or twelve meals that are excellent and then one that is not quite up to snuff. He will remember that one and pan the restaurant, forgetting that even in his own home he can prepare a meal that is a bust.

Further, the most celebrated critics in New York are well known to the restaurant as well as to the public. In short, we see them coming, recognize them, and break our necks to try to please them.

Another reason why I feel that the opinions of food critics are invalid is that personal taste enters into the critique. For example, some critics do not like fish, and yet they will go into a fish restaurant, dine, and then write their opinion. Decor, sentimental attachment, particular location, particular specialties, type of clientele, associations, and a feeling of well-being must all be considered. A sixty-year-old bachelor, a seventy-year-old dowager, a thirty-year-old married couple, a young college-age couple, a Texan, a hippie, a Frenchman, a Bostonian all have very different ideas about the kind of restaurant they like.

Some people feel comfortable in unpretentious, simple places that serve good food. Others are more concerned about atmosphere. Some rate service above all, and are willing to settle for second-rate food.

Food, of course, should be the major criterion for judging any restaurant. However, even within this area tastes differ widely. For example, for years a customer came into the Colony and ordered caviar and champagne twice a week. His first trip to Europe, he said, was disappointing in only one particular sense. He had eaten caviar in Rome, Paris, and Copenhagen, but it wasn't as good as that he had had at the Colony. It didn't appeal to his taste because it tasted different. All imported caviar has preservative added to it. The caviar in Europe, the best and the one that sells at a premium, has no preservative in it. This man, however, had become accustomed to the taste of the added preservative.

Insofar as restaurant guides go, the *Guide Michelin* is an excellent directive—but only when you are dining in Europe. Since the restaurants are visited four or five times a year, a reasonable estimate of their caliber is presented. However, when the Michelin people came to this country, they paid one visit to each restaurant and then rated them. Many restaurants that should have been given good ratings were not, and vice versa. The closest thing we have in this country to the *Guide Michelin* is the *Mobil Oil Guide,* which is reasonable in its evaluations.

Food editors, on the other hand, can be of great assistance to the cook. But when they glamorize the cooking of food, they become ludicrous. Cooking is hard work. Granted, it can be fun, it can be therapy, but it is nonetheless hard work. The late Clementine Paddleford was my idea of the perfect food editor. She never surrounded cooking with an aura of mystery or glamor. She appreciated adaptation of classic dishes and understood the problems that restaurants face in producing good food.

Poppy Cannon is a bit more elaborate, but I think she is excellent. She is not way out; she writes well, and she sticks to the facts.

One prominent food editor, however, is not my cup of tea. In the first place, most of his recipes are too involved. He has nothing to do but cook, and can spend six hours fiddling around in the kitchen to produce a dinner for two. A restaurant must conversely produce over two hundred dinners, all different and all good. The average person can do neither. In addition, he has a habit of telling people what they should eat and where they should eat. I think he is very pretentious.

Another food editor writes so sourly about restaurants

that I can only conclude that there aren't any good restaurants in New York City. Perhaps he was correct in his blast at the Colony, but what are his bases for criticism? And further, how is *he* qualified to pick apart, one by one, all the restaurants in the city that try to maintain standards of elegance and excellence despite an ever increasingly difficult situation? We were all viciously abused. The man was vindictive, and one can only assume that his articles were personal vendettas resulting from a bad experience in the restaurant business.

Recently for *New York* magazine a food critic visited a half dozen of New York's finest and most expensive restaurants to see how cheaply she could eat in each one. This was absurd. Why on earth go to restaurants that are world famous for their food, elegance, service, and atmosphere and try to get off cheaply? If that is what you have in mind, you're better off staying at home and cooking your own dinner.

And this brings me to the subject of cookbooks. Most of them are useless, for the simple reason that you can't make half the recipes included. Many require rare herbs or items unavailable in the average kitchen or supermarket. To cook from most cookbooks requires a kitchen completely stocked with well over five hundred different items.

Because most cookbooks are written by people who go from place to place collecting recipes from restaurants, the recipes are rarely adapted for the home kitchen. If they are tested, it is in elaborate kitchens by professionals. Since the fires are hotter, the pots are copper, and hundreds of items and gadgets are readily available, the recipe as written will rarely turn out the way it should.

In addition, most cookbooks are not written for the busy homemaker. Many are written for the male hobbyist who will take the time to prepare elaborate dishes because he cooks only on weekends. To a housewife with three or four children and a husband to cook for day in and day out, nothing could be more boring than such cooking. And there just isn't the time to create a culinary *pièce de résistance* on a whim.

Most gourmet cookbooks are far too involved. One can be inspired by beautiful full-color photographs, and no doubt these are very challenging to the person who has the time and money to cook for a hobby. However, many of these recipes should actually be handled only by a first-rate chef or a professional cook.

If you do use these cookbooks, always try the recipe out on the family first. Then, if you like it, serve it to company. You will save yourself a great deal of time and possibly avoid a disaster.

The cookbooks that I recommend are *The Perfect Hostess* and *The Joy of Cooking. The Perfect Hostess* is well written and lists all methods of preparation step by step. Almost all recommended ingredients are available in any supermarket. Most of them are actually staples that most people have in their kitchens. *The Joy of Cooking* includes a section devoted to cooking terminology and learning how to cook. The sections on cooking equipment and on practical good housekeeping are indispensable to the new bride on a limited budget. I also recommend the *Good House-keeping Cookbook* for lucid and practical cooking information. Each of its recipes has been tested by my wife and me in our home kitchen, and we found that they have been adapted to the average homemaker's kitchen.

Magazine recipes are also very helpful and are reasonably acquired. A woman sitting under the drier at the beauty parlor can pick up *McCall's* or the *Ladies' Home Journal*, jot down a recipe, do the shopping, and then go home and cook something her family has never had before.

In addition, a good deal must be said for the inexpensive home magazines that are available in supermarkets.

There are many good seasonal and holiday recipes available in them. They're fairly simple to execute, and most of the ingredients can be purchased right there in the same supermarket.

TV cooking, especially Julia Child's show, is very helpful as well as being great fun to view. Not only do you watch the preparation step by step, but you also see the finished product. Perhaps the one drawback is that frequent claim is made that the entire meal can be put together in half an hour. This is utter nonsense. Note that all the ingredients are peeled, diced, and sliced beforehand. The butter and oil are always at the correct temperature. If you try one of the recipes, you may well find that the half hour becomes three hours before you turn out the dish.

And never try to dice or slice the way the pros do it on TV. It is a good way to lose three fingers unless you know exactly what you are doing.

On radio, the McCanns on Station WOR in New York are excellent on food. They talk about it in a level-headed way and offer their public many ideas about the simple preparation of reasonable dishes. They also discuss marketing values and foreign food. I think they are quite probably the best advisers in the business.

The public has always been something to cope with, and although "the customer is always right," I feel that on occasion the customer is irrevocably wrong. Please understand that the following is not a gripe session. I merely wish to give you more understanding of what a restaurant owner must face day in and day out in dealing with his customers. Perhaps your greater understanding will help you to enjoy dining out to a greater extent.

First of all, there is the customer whom I refer to as the "Imposer." This customer seemed to feel that in my position as owner of the Colony I should have been at his beck and call to perform a myriad of services. At times, of

Never try to dice or slice the way the pros do it on TV. It's a good way to lose three fingers unless you know what you're doing.

course, out of friendship I did certain favors. However, the list of impositions was staggering.

For instance, a lady came in one afternoon and told me that she had to leave for the country within the hour. She asked me to pick up her daughter, who was coming down from boarding school, at Grand Central and to deliver her safely to her sister-in-law's apartment.

People have called me and asked if I would please send my chef up to their apartment to cook dinner, never realizing that I pay my chef to cook in my restaurant for my clientele.

The classic imposition occurred several years ago, when a man came in and asked me if I would do him the favor of buying his wife a present the following day. He was leaving for Japan that evening.

I agreed. The man wanted his wife to have a Mustang. When I inquired what kind, the man said, "I'll leave that to you." He also failed to provide the money to pay for the car.

I picked out a car, paid four thousand dollars for it out of my own pocket, and had it delivered. Shortly thereafter, the man's wife called and said she didn't like the color. When the man returned, he confronted me with, "What do you mean, spending four thousand dollars of my money for a car that my wife doesn't like?" I recognized that the situation was totally unreasonable, but told him that I would bring it back and try to make some kind of deal. Fortunately the dealer accepted the car and exchanged it for one in the color the lady wanted.

In addition, I was constantly prevailed upon to arrange for hotel reservations, theater tickets, airline tickets, babysitters, interior decorators, TV sets; to remind husbands of anniversaries; to get people through customs and to get children into quality schools. Customers took it for granted that I could and should perform all of these favors.

The "Small Fry" are people who either through misinformation, a cloying sense of inferiority, or just sheer contrariness insist on sitting at a particular table. For some inane reason, they feel that somehow or other they will gain social prestige and significance by being seen at a certain location in the restaurant. Unfortunately, they don't seem to realize that it isn't the table that makes a person important: it is the other way around.

In fact, many of the Colony's most distinguished visitors always insisted on being seated in the very locations the "Small Fry" considered undesirable. The entire concept of "prime tables" is generally laughed at by the great restaurateurs of the world.

At the Colony, the bar had become "the" place to dine. Actually, the bar was not only cramped but noisy; the dining room was far more gracious and pleasant to dine in. People slowly came around to this realization. I was often amused at how I could manipulate my customers by employing reverse psychology. I would tell a patron that the dining room was jammed. The customer invariably switched gears and insisted on sitting in the dining room rather than in the bar.

Every now and then, undesirable guests who were vulgar, loud, or impossibly drunk came into the Colony. If that was the case, we usually got rid of them immediately. On the other hand, if they got disorderly after being seated, the situation was always ticklish. Other guests became outraged and disgusted. About the only thing that could be done in this situation was to try to displease these people. Hopefully, after a while they would get the hint and leave. If they didn't, I courteously asked them to go.

Often someone would come into the Colony once or twice and then pull the personal touch; that is, he would confide all the intimate details of his life to me. Subsequently, he felt, this should make him a member of an

The "Small Fry" are people who either through misinformation, a cloying sense of inferiority, or just sheer contrariness insist on sitting at a particular table. For some inane reason, they feel that somehow they will gain social prestige and significance by being seen at a certain location in the restaurant.

"in" group of customers, and he would expect the same kind of highly personal attention and interest as someone who had been dining regularly at the Colony for twenty or thirty years.

Almost all restaurateurs suffer from the "Familiar Face," the customer who comes in and says, "Don't you remember me? I was in with Mr. Jones six months ago." If recognition is not forthcoming and it is explained that since the man was in several thousand other people have come in also, he is offended.

The ladies sometimes created problems for us. They can and do change their clothes as drastically as their moods. Fortunately, a restaurateur has only to cope with their costume changes. Their husbands manage their moods. For example, a lady might come in at lunchtime wearing sunglasses and a simple hairdo. Several days later, the same lady would come in wearing evening clothes and an elaborate wig and look like a totally different woman. She would inevitably be offended if I didn't recognize her.

Drink orders often provided a good laugh for us at the Colony. There was one gentleman who came in and always ordered a very, very dry martini. After several months of experience in serving this man his drink, I had instructed the waiters to serve him straight gin. He always returned the drink, claiming that it wasn't dry enough. The drink was returned to the bar, and then the same drink was brought back to his table. The gentleman would always say, "Ah, this is superb."

The fresh-fruit-juice nuts are also amusing. They will always insist that the fruit juice that goes into their drinks be freshly squeezed. In any quality restaurant, ONLY fresh fruit juice is put in the drinks. It is unnecessary to request this.

Reservations have always contributed their share of difficulty, and many customers are totally unreasonable about this situation. Often they would call and reserve a table for 9:00 P.M. They would arrive punctually and expect to sit down immediately to eat, but sometimes this was simply impossible.

If, for example, a couple who had come in at 7:00 P.M. were seated at the table reserved for the 9:00 P.M. party and then took much longer than the average two hours for dinner, it was naturally quite out of order to ask them to leave. Seating plans had to be reshuffled at the last minute to accommodate the 9:00 P.M. party. A table cannot be kept empty all evening just for one particular 9:00 P.M. party. A restaurant depends on the income from two or three servings in order to survive financially.

"The Loser" is another customer we had to cope with. Many patrons insisted that they had lost this or that at the Colony. In 95 percent of all cases, the missing articles turned up elsewhere. One evening a lady came in with a party of eight. During the dessert she clutched at her neck and realized that she did not have her ruby necklace on. Immediately she called me over and insisted that she had lost her jewels in the restaurant. I advised her to go to the ladies' room to see if perhaps the jewels had slipped off her neck into her dress. She returned and said the eighty-thousand-dollar jewels weren't there.

The floor, lobby, and the ladies' room were searched, but to no avail. While the search was going on, I told the lady that I did not notice the necklace on her when she came in. Her companions all insisted that she did indeed have it on. It was decided to wait until the following day to take any serious action. The next morning the lady called and said she had forgotten to put her necklace on and that she had found it on her dressing table. She didn't even have the grace to apologize for her mistake.

There were also guests who insisted on keeping the waiter and captain for their very own personal use. The minute they tended to someone else, these customers created a fuss because they felt they weren't getting proper attention. Waiters in public restaurants are not personal butlers. They are responsible for tending to several groups of diners and cannot possibly center all their attention on one table. Captains are responsible for even more guests and can spend even less time with each individual diner.

The "Demander" is another type of customer who

wreaks havoc with the waiters. He continually and systematically makes service requests. If it isn't water, it's butter, or salt, or a sharp knife, or ice, or bread. He never allows the waiter a chance to perform the service himself without being asked.

In addition, he will make requests of anyone passing by and will often end up with four salt shakers, three butters—in short, two or three times as much of everything as he needs.

By keeping the waiter constantly running, and by interrupting his serving of food, the customer inevitably ends up on the short end of the stick. His service will be slow and there will be confusion. Following such an experience, the "Demander" will complain bitterly that the service was bad, and that he had to ask for everything that appeared on his table.

Another thorn in my side was the would-be expert who would discuss the entire operation of a dining room with the waiter, captain, and management during his dinner. If his shoulder of lamb was not on the table in ten minutes, he would complain that I didn't know how to operate my restaurant.

If I explained to this man that the food passed through fifteen hands on its way to the table, and that it took twenty minutes to cook his shoulder of lamb, he would become abusive. The same man will wait three or four weeks for a suit from his tailor, but will complain bitterly if he must wait twenty-five minutes for a superb dinner.

In the same area, there is the "Rejector." There is nothing more irritating to a restaurateur than a customer who sends something back to the kitchen with the words, "This is no good!" Of course there are times when food is improperly prepared, and it should be sent back to the kitchen. However, when it really is a matter of personal taste, the words, "I believe I have made a mistake. I don't really feel like eating this. Could I please have something else?" are certainly preferred. At the Colony, we would always change the order with great pleasure.

Some customers have the impression that the more hell they raise, the better the service and food will be. Being overly fussy is an American "thing" in restaurants, but it is distinctly the wrong tactic. If there are complaints, report them to the manager sincerely and honestly. You can be assured that all that is humanly possible will be done to correct them, if they are legitimate.

Actually, chronic complaining will eventually work against a customer. Although the personnel of any restaurant are there to serve you, and although the smile and politesse will never vanish, rest assured there is a limit to human endurance. There are dozens of little tricks any waiter or captain can pull to guarantee you a miserable meal.

In contrast to the chronic complainer, there is the customer who will grin and bear anything and everything. Remember that a restaurant and a staff exist to please you. If the food is not quite right, or if the service is sloppy, by all means discreetly call it to the attention of the captain or the manager. He will do his best to rectify the situation. Constructive criticism is a vital part of the restaurant business and is always welcome.

Occasionally, of course, mistakes are made in the preparation or serving of food. This is only human. Do not hesitate to mention it. Restaurant men are quite aware that this can and does happen and often sample food before it is brought to a table. In addition, a knowledgeable restaurant man watches every table. If he notices that a customer is picking at his food or that he isn't eating it, he will voluntarily ask if anything is wrong or if the customer would prefer to order something else.

Another "button lip" with whom we had to cope was the customer who came in and when asked if he needed

Occasionally, of course, mistakes are made in the preparation or serving of food.

help would reply, "No, I'm just waiting for someone."
Ten minutes later, to a second such inquiry his reply
would be the same. It generally turned out that the person
he was to meet had already been seated. Inevitably, the
customer would say upon meeting his friend, "Nobody
told me you were here."

If you go into a restaurant, introduce yourself to the
headwaiter and say, "I am Mr. Jones. I am waiting for Mr.
Smith. Has he arrived yet?"

Since dinner at the Colony was expensive, we often
ran into the price controller, the man who decided what
the prices in my restaurant should have been. He would
complain that high prices are an injustice. He never realized that these prices were not arrived at arbitrarily. Every
restaurant must make a reasonable profit, and maintaining standards of elegance and excellence costs money. The
best is always expensive.

This man would often add up the price of everything
on the bill and then accuse the restaurant of cheating him.
Obviously, any restaurant with as fine a reputation as the
Colony had stands to gain absolutely nothing by trying to
cheat someone out of two or three dollars. It would be
sheer stupidity to endanger a fifty-year-old reputation of
taste and elegance for the sake of a few dollars.

People who received bills for $150 would often com-
plain about the price of the food. They neglected to
consider that their bar bill—including items such as champagne, brandy cocktails, and fine wines—could comprise
two-thirds of the total amount of the bill.

Another type of customer concerned with prices is the
thrift nut. "One spinach, one salad, one entrée with two
plates, two forks, and two knives," believe it or not, was an
occasional request. If saving money is your thing, don't
go to any top-quality restaurant. Not only does it look
cheap to the restaurant and the help, but you'll feel pretty

cheap yourself. Furthermore, dining in a fine restaurant should be an occasion for happiness and good times, not a time to worry about splitting servings to save money.

Some customers would ask for one order of a salad or vegetable because they felt two orders were too much for them to eat. In a quality restaurant, the waiter will tell you if one order is enough for two persons.

"Why charge for the bread, butter, celery, and radishes?" asked many customers. Unfortunately, good celery, bread, butter, and radishes cost money. Fine linen tablecloths and napkins are expensive to maintain and launder. This cost must be covered.

To add these costs to the price of an entrée or dessert would have caused immediate and resentful reaction among my steady customers; hence the B & B charge. I believed that there should be no hidden charges and that a customer should know exactly what he is paying for.

Steak hounds were our nemesis. The Colony kitchen, staffed by eighty-four people, was prepared to cook just about any kind of classic cuisine imaginable. Yet scores of people would come in for dinner and order steak, salad, and potatoes. Incidentally, that number includes a recent President's daughter.

From a restaurant's point of view, steak is the item that brings in the least profit. A notable restaurant in Boston has ordered their waiters, captains, and staff to discourage customers from ordering steak. In fact, each time an order is taken, the employee pays $1.50 to the management.

From the diner's point of view, why on earth go to one of the finest restaurants in the world and order a piece of meat that can be prepared in thousands of other places, or even in your own kitchen? It just doesn't make sense to pass up the delicacy and delight of classic cuisine for a piece of red meat.

Another kind of order we discouraged came from the wise guy. Believe it or not, there were people who came into the Colony and ordered Chinese food. To discourage this practice, we sent out for it and charged the customer about four times what he would normally pay for the food.

We found ungracious guests particularly offensive. How often have you entertained friends or business associates for dinner or luncheon and had to endure a steady stream of criticism of the food or service in the restaurant? These same people would never open their mouths to complain if they were dining in your home and something was not to their liking. However, when in a restaurant, they feel they have the prerogative of embarrassing the host by complaining.

Such complaints are the option of the host and not of the guests. The host has tried to entertain nicely and to so complain is very rude.

Another highly offensive kind of patron is the "Chimney." People who eat their dinner with a cigarette in hand are very discouraging. First of all, it is a breach of good manners and intolerably inconsiderate of other people at the table. And then, the same man who smokes a pack of cigarettes during dinner will almost always be the most severe critic of the food. How can he taste it?

Occasionally we run into the "Voice of Doom." There are customers who do not feel comfortable in a restaurant unless it is totally jammed, with the noise level just short of discotheque decibel rate.

Often on a slow night when leisurely, civilized dining was possible, customers of this sort would approach me with, "Business not so hot these days, huh, Gene?" and then later they would say to their friends, "The Colony is going downhill. The other night we were in and the place was like a tomb."

The steady customer was always a welcome sight at the

Colony, but beyond two or three visits a week this kind of customer became very difficult to please. I didn't like to see my patrons fall into a rut, and found that if they visited other restaurants and had some basis for comparison, they appreciated the Colony more.

On the other hand, the uninitiated and inexperienced American diner's most common fault is his antagonism. He feels he will not receive the attention that is his due if he is not known in a certain restaurant. He will most likely enter with a chip on his shoulder, fearful that he is going to be taken. The manager, captain, and waiters are there to fight with him, and he must battle his way through every request to have an enjoyable meal. More often than not, this diner will abuse the waiters. In Europe a waiter is rarely abused. He is a man of prestige, and the service he renders is appreciated and respected. He is not ordered around disrespectfully as so often occurs in this country.

It is certainly not to anyone's credit to pull this act. It reveals a lack of sophistication as well as atrocious manners and bad breeding. This attitude can only be explained by the average American's lack of experience in dining out. Families who spend a great deal of time in restaurants and feel at home in them know how they operate and understand why this approach is wrong. They realize that you don't have to be rude to get what you want. They know that a quality restaurant will try to please you, since they want you to repeat your visit.

Finally, and without question, the most impossible kind of patron is the individual who is bored and jaded. There is nothing on earth that anyone can do to please this person.

CHAPTER FOUR

Household Hints

A *is for Asparagus, and it's also for Advice. I owned one of the finest kitchens in the Western World, but am equally at home in my kitchen at home. My years of experience in both areas have given me much practical education in the preparation of food. This chapter offers the amateur chef, housewife, or hobbyist a series of straight-from-the-shoulder household hints I have picked up over those years.*

Asparagus
The king of vegetables, dethroned by the American cook. The reason? Overcooking! Try cutting down on the cooking

time by a quarter to a third and learn what asparagus really tastes like.

Barbecued Onions

At our house, a specialty. Take red or blue onions and bury them in the barbecue coals. When they're done, take them out, peel off the outside crust, and you'll enjoy a sweet treat with no aftertaste. Be sure to get red or blue onions.

Bacon

When you buy bacon, be certain that it isn't too lean. Bacon SHOULD have a lot of fat on it.

Bread

In America and in Europe, two different concepts: America's bland horror, Europe's taste treat. If convenient, try some of the more exotic varieties available in ethnic neighborhoods. Worth the trouble of making the trip.

Cake Mixes

A miracle. Some are good, some bad. It's up to you to try them all and find out which is best for you. One more way to get mother out of the kitchen.

Carving

Most people don't know what they're doing. Get good instructions from a book and practice. You can ruin a good roast by cutting in the wrong direction. Always use a sharp knife.

Cheese

Americans are becoming more and more sophisticated in this area, and as the market grows, more and more of Europe's superb cheeses are becoming available. Try them all: Petit Suisse, Gourmandaise, Brie, and on and on. When you cut cheese, put a drop of olive oil or water on the knife and see the difference in cutting ease.

Chinese Food

Why not adapt Chinese vegetables to traditional cuisine?

Coffee

Remember that coffee can and will turn rancid after only a few days if proper care has not been taken. Never put coffee in a metal container. The seams of the container trap old coffee turned rancid that will subsequently turn the new coffee rancid rapidly. Use a glass container that has been thoroughly washed. Buy only small quantities of coffee at a time. The longer you keep it, the worse it will taste. To make superb coffee, use a lot of grounds. Skimping here is insane, as you will only come out with something tasting like dishwater. If instructions call for two tablespoons per cup, put in three. In our kitchen at home, the coffee container in the pot is always filled to the brim. Always use fresh cold water.

Duck

Duck must have a lot of fat on it, for the fat is what makes the duck crisp.

Electric Bread Baskets

Sensational invention. It keeps the bread and rolls warm and helps the hostess to synchronize everything. It also allows her to spend more time with her guests.

Electric Carving Knives

Another miracle. Superb for slicing but not so good for cutting meat off the bones. They were not used at the Colony Restaurant because they are unprofessional, but they are used in our household.

Electric Hot Trays
Also sensational. You should have several. Everything can
be cooked before and kept warm on trays. Again the hostess
is given more time with her family and guests.

Electric Stoves
At the Colony, gas was used, but our stove at home is electric. It is cleaner, easier to keep clean, and there is no dan-
ger of leaking gas. Electricity is quicker than gas. There is
a difference in the cooking time, so cookbooks should always indicate whether the food was tested on a gas or electric stove.

Enameled Pots and Cookware
Good in the oven, but not so hot on the burner because of
uneven heat.

Fat
Pork, veal, and lamb should have a lot of fat. Fat helps to
hold the meat together, improves the taste, and keeps the
meat moist.

Frozen Meat
You can cook this with great success immediately after removing from the freezer. A steak, for example, should be
placed in a very hot grill, seared thoroughly on both sides so
that the juice can't leak out, and then cooked slowly. It will
come to the table tasty and full of juice.

Frozen Vegetables
Almost a way of life today. Some say that fresh is the only
kind to cook, but with the advances in preservation and
flash freezing, there is little difference between fresh and
frozen. Naturally, fresh vegetables were used at the Colony,
but at home we use frozen. Doctor these up with salt, pepper,
butter, Tabasco, or any spices you wish to experiment with.

Fruit

Keep in mind that fresh fruit arrives at your grocer unripe and green. It ripens in the store or at home. Therefore, if you are buying a melon, select one that is just on the brink of turning bad, or buy it several days ahead of time and permit it to ripen at home. Then you will have the flavor you expect. A pear that is just a little brown will be a delicious treat, far better than the picture of perfection, which generally is as hard as a rock.

Garlic

If you want garlic flavor, get a garlic press, place a clove of garlic in the press, and squeeze out one or two drops into the food. In this way, you don't eat small pieces of garlic. For French dressing, one or two drops are ENOUGH! When you cook lamb, put the garlic in the meat so that it can be removed. Use very little and be sure that it is very fresh. Don't keep garlic around the house, as it gets stale.

Hamburger

Use cheap hamburger meat, as it isn't too fatty. First-class meat has to be fatty in order to be good. If you chop it up, it becomes fatty hamburger and not too appetizing. In addition, it is a crime to chop up good meat.

Knives

A cheap knife is only slightly better than no knife at all. You can't sharpen it and it makes a mess out of anything you wish to cut. A good set of knives should run around twenty-five to thirty dollars. They will last a lifetime if given proper care. Use them only for the specific jobs they were created for. Keep them sharp. Steel knives will discolor, but they are more serviceable in the long run than the stainless varieties. Never wash any knife in the dishwasher, as the edge will be ruined. The temperature is also too high. Wash them by hand and care for them scrupulously. At home my good knives are kept in a special closet under lock and key!

Meat Thermometers
Essential. Every piece of meat is different. The same amount of time can leave one roast rare, another overdone. A meat thermometer removes any risk whatsoever.

Mint
Dry mint is one of the few spices that can be stored for several years without losing its potency.

Mixing Machines for Kneading Dough
There's one in my home kitchen, but I am frank to admit that I have never been successful with it.

Mustard
Buy prepared mustards in small quantities, as mustard loses its flavor rapidly once it has been opened and stored in the refrigerator. Dry mustard can be bought in large quantities; it doesn't lose its flavor.

Oysters
"R" months? Hogwash! The old wives' tale that oysters are good only in months with an "R" in them is not true. Oysters are good any time of the year. One would think that the oyster industry would stage some kind of advertising campaign to inform the public of this ridiculous misconception. It undoubtedly came about before the days of modern refrigeration and quick transport. Oysters are just as good in summer as in winter.

Pepper
Always use freshly ground pepper. Get yourself a pepper mill and some corns and grind away. The taste is fresh,

pungent. and heady compared to that of the bland packaged ground variety.

Pots

Copper is best. Copper-bottomed pots are acceptable, but the heat is not distributed around the sides as with the use of full copper pots.

Refrigerator

KEEP IT CLEAN! WASH IT OUT EVERY TEN DAYS! Food picks up odors or aromas in no time. A marvelous dinner prepared in advance can be ruined by storage in a foul, rancid-ridden refrigerator. Have you ever had a nice, tall gin and tonic chilled with ice cubes that taste and smell of mildew? Need more be said? Keep the refrigerator cold. Never leave the door open, not even for a minute. At home we have four refrigerators—one for food, another for beer, soft drinks, and wines, a third for glasses, mugs, and wine glasses, and one freezer.

Rice

Rice, like almost everything else in this country, is always overcooked. If you prepare and eat it immediately it may be passable, but if you let it stand for ten or fifteen minutes it tastes like paste. Good rice is imported, very expensive. A commercial brand that I recommend is Uncle Ben's, but it must be undercooked. Rice should be served like spaghetti, al dente, with a little bite to it. At the Colony we use rice grown on our own farm in Italy. It is different from American rice. It is also better.

Salad Bowls

Simple, big, and wooden is the rule. Forget the varnished, shellacked, designed horrors. Never wash your salad bowl under hot water as it brings the oil out. Never wash it with soap. Wash it in cold water and dry it with a paper towel. It will never turn rancid if you follow these simple instructions.

Cute little salad bowls are ridiculous and impractical. You cannot make a decent salad by pouring dressing on top of some greens sitting in a mini-bowl. Try and mix it! Everything falls out. Mix it in a large bowl and then serve it on a LARGE plate.

Salad Dressing
Pour it on just before you serve the salad unless you use garlic. In that case, pour it on several minutes before, so that the salad can absorb the dressing.

Salt
So basic and yet so abused in this country. Most Americans don't even put salt in soup when they make it. Consequently, American men, immediately upon sitting down at a table, automatically salt their food. Barbaric! You should at least taste it before salting. Many good dishes can be ruined by putting salt upon salt. New Yorkers tend to be more sophisticated in this area, but the rest of the country still clings to this philistine habit. Furthermore, probably the one time when salt shouldn't be used, it is poured on. Never salt meat before putting it on the broiler. It makes the meat tough. Always salt upon removing.

Skillets
Enameled skillets don't distribute the heat. If you have a large burner you're safe with enamel, but if you have a small burner, forget it.

Cast-iron and copper skillets are the best because the heat radiates. Of the two, copper is better because it heats evenly. Cast iron takes a long time to heat up. The butter should bounce when you put it in the skillet.

Spaghetti
I like mine cooked, placed in the refrigerator and then later fried with butter.

Spices
Spice shelf sets with thirty or forty jars full of every conceivable kind of spice may look very nice, but they are definitely not practical. Most of the spices contained are used rarely and consequently will be impotent after six months. Buy fresh spices every six months or so, and never mix the new with the old. Throw the old away.

Sauce
Never leave a sauce alone. Watch it like a hawk, as it will stick and burn, which will affect the taste. Stir constantly with a wooden spoon—for one hundred years, if necessary.

Stew
Stew is always better the next day, and improves each day after that. Make a stew for Monday-night dinner, but make enough to enjoy it the following Saturday. That's when it's at the peak of its flavor.

Tea
If you want colored water, use one tea bag per cup. If you want tea, use two. At the Colony, five or six tea bags went into making every pot of tea. You may think this is extravagant, but then anything that is good is extravagant.

Teflon
This is good for dieters because you don't have to use oil or butter to cook in.

Vegetables
Here again, Americans overcook. No wonder the "meat and potatoes" tradition has evolved. Vegetables should be crisp

and yet tender. Try cutting down on the cooking time given
on package directions and in recipes.

Wire Whisks
A rarity in the American household, but absolutely indispensable. Mix sauces, eggs, etc., with one of these, then see
and taste the difference.

Wooden Spoons
Always mix with a wooden spoon. Wash it under hot water.
Do not use soap. Buy a lot of them. You'll need them.

CHAPTER FIVE

Recipes

APPETIZERS

Crêpes Farcis Colony
Canapés Arno
Quiche Lorraine Colony
Foies de Volaille en Brochette with Beurre Café
Mozzarella in Carrozza
Sma Kottbullar (Swedish Meatballs)

CRÊPES FARCIS COLONY

8 Suzette pancakes
16 shrimps, cooked and shelled
4 tablespoons lump crab meat
Butter
Curry sauce
Mustard sauce

Dice rather finely your shrimps and lump crab meat. Then melt some butter in a saucepan and add the shrimps and crab meat. Sauté for approximately two minutes and then add curry sauce to the preparation and cook to boiling point. Do not boil as preparation will curdle. Be certain to stir the ingredients well when the curry sauce has been added.

Place your pancakes in an open-face position in front of you. Place approximately two tablespoons of your preparation in the center of each pancake, then fold and roll the pancakes until they are tubular in shape. Cut the outer edges of the pancakes, heat, and serve.

Serve both curry sauce and mustard sauce with each portion of crêpes, placing the sauces next to each pancake, one sauce on each side. Serves 4.

The flavoring of the crêpes can be altered to suit individual taste. Some people prefer to add 2 tablespoons of white wine to the sauces; others enjoy the sweet taste of curaçao. This recipe is not ironbound in its manner of preparation. For example, some people are not fond of shrimp, so in lieu of shrimp one could use lobster.

CANAPÉS ARNO

1 slice bread
1 cooked lobster tail
½ pound parsley
1 soupspoon mustard sauce

On a piece of fresh toast, place slices of cooked lobster. Cover with fresh parsley and place under the broiler until the parsley is well crisped. Serve with mustard sauce. Serves 1.

QUICHE LORRAINE COLONY

1 pound short paste
3 ounces smoked bacon, finely diced
½ medium onion, chopped
4 ounces Swiss cheese, finely diced
3 eggs
Salt, pepper and nutmeg
1 cup heavy cream
2 cups milk

Line a tart plate with a good short paste. Make some cuts in the dough with a knife. Put in the oven and bake until the paste turns to a golden brown. Remove and cover the paste with smoked bacon and chopped onions that have been previously cooked. To this add Swiss cheese.

Pour over these ingredients a custard made as follows: Beat 3 eggs very well with a fork; add salt, pepper and nutmeg. To this mixture add 2 cups of milk and 1 cup of heavy cream and blend well.

Place the pie in a moderately heated oven (300° F.) and bake for approximately 30 minutes.

Remove and serve hot. Serves 4.

FOIES de VOLAILLE
en BROCHETTE

6 to 8 slices bacon
2 pounds chicken livers
1 6-ounce can broiled-in-butter mushroom caps
1 7-ounce can water chestnuts
Warmed brandy or Cointreau

Cut bacon slices into 1-inch pieces. Cut large chicken livers in fourths, smaller ones in halves or thirds. Drain mushrooms and water chestnuts. On cocktail picks alternate bacon, chicken liver, mushrooms, water chestnuts, and bacon. Repeat until all ingredients are used. Place in foil-lined broiler pan without rack. Brush with Beurre Café. Broil 3 inches below source of heat until bacon is crisp and chicken livers done (6 to 8 minutes). Turn often, brushing each time with sauce. When done, flambé with warmed brandy or Cointreau. Serves 4.

BEURRE CAFÉ

¼ *cup butter*
½ *cup strong coffee*
2 *drops angostura bitters*
2 *tablespoons brown sugar*

Melt butter in small saucepan. Add coffee, bitters, and sugar and stir until sugar dissolves. Keep hot for basting. Serves 4.

MOZZARELLA IN CARROZZA

8 large slices firm-textured white bread, ½ inch thick
4 slices mozzarella cheese
2 eggs, beaten
1 tablespoon oil
1 tablespoon butter
Fresh parsley sprigs

With a sharp knife, remove crusts from bread. On each of 4 slices of the bread place a slice of mozzarella. Top with another slice of bread. If necessary, trim excess bread to make a neat sandwich. In a shallow dish, beat eggs. Dip each sandwich in the beaten egg, turning to coat lightly on both sides. In heavy skillet, heat oil and butter. Add sandwiches. Cook until golden brown on both sides. Drain on absorbent paper. Remove to serving dish and garnish with sprigs of fresh parsley. Serves 4.

Mozzarella slices may be topped by a thin slice of prosciutto ham or two fillets of anchovies.

SMA KOTTBULLAR
(Swedish Meatballs)

3 tablespoons butter
4 tablespoons finely chopped onion
1 cup mashed boiled potato
3 tablespoons fine dry bread crumbs
1 pound lean ground beef
⅓ cup heavy cream
1 teaspoon salt
1 egg
1 tablespoon finely chopped fresh parsley (optional)
2 tablespoons vegetable oil
1 tablespoon flour
¾ cup light or heavy cream

In a small frying pan, melt 1 tablespoon of butter over moderate heat. When the foam subsides, add the onions and cook for about 5 minutes, until they are soft and translucent but not brown.

In a large bowl, combine the onions, mashed potato, bread crumbs, meat, cream, salt, egg, and parsley (if desired). Knead vigorously with both hands or beat with a wooden spoon until all the ingredients are well blended and the mixture is smooth and fluffy. Shape into small balls about 1 inch in diameter. Arrange the meatballs in one layer on a baking sheet or a flat tray, cover them with plastic wrap, and chill for at least 1 hour before cooking.

Over high heat, melt 2 tablespoons of butter and 2 tablespoons of oil in a heavy 10- to 12-inch skillet. When the foam subsides, add the meatballs, 8 to 10 at a time. Reduce the heat to moderate and fry the balls on all sides, shaking the pan almost constantly to roll the balls around in the hot fat to help keep their shape. In 8 to 10 minutes the meat-balls should be brown outside and show no trace of pink inside when one is broken open with a knife. Add more butter and oil to the skillet as needed, and transfer each finished batch to a casserole or baking dish and keep warm in a 200°F. oven. Serves 6 to 8 (about 50 meatballs).

If the meatballs are to be served as a main course with noodles or potatoes, you may want to make a sauce with the pan juice. Remove from the heat, pour off all the fat from the pan, and stir in 1 tablespoon of flour. Quickly stir in ¾ cup of light or heavy cream and boil the sauce over moderate heat for 2 or 3 minutes, stirring constantly, until it is thick and smooth. Pour over the meatballs and serve.

If the meatballs are to be served as an hors d'oeuvre or as part of a smorgasbord, they should be cooked as above but formed into smaller balls and served without the sauce.

SOUPS

Mille Fanti Soup Colony
Purée of Cucumber Soup Colony
Madras Soup Colony
Cream of Artichoke Soup Colony (Béchamel Sauce)
Potage Santé Colony
Consommé Printanier
Waterbury

MILLE FANTI
SOUP COLONY

2 *eggs, well beaten*
2 *tablespoons bread crumbs*
2 *tablespoons freshly grated Parmesan cheese*
1 *quart beef or chicken consommé*
Salt and pepper to taste

Beat eggs thoroughly; blend in bread crumbs, Parmesan cheese, salt and pepper. Heat consommé and keep simmering gently on the stove. Gradually pour in egg mixture, stirring briskly with a wire whisk. Then cover the pot, reduce flame, and simmer gently from 7 to 8 minutes longer. Before serving, stir again with the whisk and, if desired, sprinkle with additional grated Parmesan cheese. Serves 4.

PURÉE OF CUCUMBER
SOUP COLONY

2 *medium-size onions, finely diced*
2 *small, firm cucumbers*
4 *tablespoons butter*
4 *tablespoons flour*
1 *quart milk**
2 *tablespoons chervil leaves*
¼ *cup watercress leaves*
1 *tablespoon cornstarch*
Salt and pepper to taste

In a pot, melt 3 tablespoons butter. Dice onions finely and
fry them gently until golden. Without removing skin, cut
one cucumber in paper-thin slices and add to onions. When
cucumber begins to take color, sprinkle with flour and
continue cooking. Gradually add 1 quart milk. Season with
salt and pepper to taste and simmer for 10 minutes, being
careful not to boil. Finely dice the other cucumber and add
to the soup. In a very little amount of water cook chervil
and watercress leaves for 3 minutes. Drain and run through
a blender, or press through a strainer. Add to the soup. If a
thicker consistency is desired, dilute a tablespoon of cornstarch in a small quantity of soup, then add to the pot and
let cook for a while. Serves 4.

* *1 pint beef stock and 1 pint water can be substituted for milk.*

MADRAS SOUP COLONY

1 *quart beef or chicken consommé*
1 *teaspoon curry powder*
2 *egg yolks*
½ *cup light cream*
1 *apple, finely diced*
Salt to taste

Stir curry powder thoroughly into consommé and place pot over low flame. With a fork, break egg yolks and blend in the cream, stirring gently. Remove pot from fire and add this mixture to the consommé. Return pot to burner and heat liquid thoroughly, being very careful not to boil it. Peel and core the apple and dice it finely. Add to the liquid; correct the seasoning. Delicious also when chilled. Serves 4.

CREAM OF ARTICHOKE
SOUP COLONY

6 large artichokes
4 tablespoons butter
2 cups thin Béchamel Sauce
2 cups milk
4 tablespoons cream
Salt and pepper to taste

After removing hard leaves and cutting off stems and tops, parboil artichokes. Clean artichoke bottoms of all leaves and chokes. Melt butter, add artichoke bottoms cut in coarse pieces and cook until tender. Add a small amount of water, if necessary, to prevent burning. Using a wooden spoon, crush artichoke bottoms, blend in Béchamel Sauce, and stir to make a smooth mixture. Scald milk, and blend it in. Season with salt and pepper to taste. Stir in cream. Serves 4.

BÉCHAMEL SAUCE (Thin)

2 tablespoons butter
2 tablespoons flour
2 cups milk
Salt and pepper to taste

Warm milk. In the top of a double boiler, over simmering water, melt butter and while stirring with an even motion blend in flour a little at a time. Continue stirring and let cook for 5 minutes, then gradually add milk and continue stirring. Cook until sauce thickens, approximately 20 minutes longer, but be careful not to boil. Season with salt and pepper to taste.

POTAGE SANTÉ COLONY

3 leeks
2 tablespoons butter
1 quart beef consommé
3 medium potatoes, peeled and diced
½ cup finely cut sorrel
½ cup light cream
2 egg yolks
Salt and pepper to taste

Mince leeks finely. In a pot melt butter, add leeks, and cook over low flame until golden. Add consommé, bring to a boil, then add potatoes and sorrel. Reduce flame and let simmer until vegetables are cooked (about 20 minutes). Turn off flame. Break egg yolks, add a tablespoon of cream to them, and stir. Add the remaining cream. Pour this mixture into the soup and stir until well blended. Serves 4.

CONSOMMÉ PRINTANIER

1 quart chicken consommé
1 carrot
1 turnip
1 tablespoon small peas
1 tablespoon small string beans
1 tablespoon asparagus tips
10 sorrel leaves
10 lettuce leaves
1 pinch small chervil leaves

Have ready one quart of chicken consommé. Cut carrot and turnip into round slices ½ inch thick. Cut these round slices into little sticks, making a sufficient number to fill 1 tablespoon with each vegetable. Cook these little sticks in consommé, and reduce the latter to a glaze.

Put the carrot and turnip sticks into the soup tureen with 1 tablespoon of small peas, the same quantity of small string beans and asparagus tips, 10 sorrel leaves, and 10 lettuce leaves, the latter being poached in some consommé. When about to serve, pour the boiling consommé over these garnishes and add a large pinch of small chervil leaves. Serves 4.

WATERBURY

1 ½ teaspoons strong curry sauce or to taste
1 cup cream
1 egg yolk

To curry sauce, add cream and egg yolk. Place in a saucepan and bring almost to a boiling point. Remove from fire and chill. Yields 1 serving.

EGGS

Poached Eggs Tourangelle Colony (Tourangelle Sauce)
Egg Custard Florentine Colony
Eggs Encore Colony (Creamed Chicken Hash and
Sauce Mornay)
Eggs Bonne Femme Colony
Eggs Mollet Portugaise Colony
Eggs with Artichoke Bottoms Colony

POACHED EGGS
TOURANGELLE COLONY

1½ pounds fresh mushrooms
4 tablespoons butter
6 ounces dry white wine
8 poached eggs
2 cups Tourangelle Sauce
Salt and pepper to taste

Brush mushrooms thoroughly under running cold water, remove stems, and reserve. Slice caps. Melt butter in a pan, add mushrooms, and sauté for 5 minutes. When they are cooked, add wine and cook until wine is almost evaporated. Season with salt and pepper. Place on serving dish and top with poached eggs, accompanied by Tourangelle Sauce. Serves 4.

TOURANGELLE SAUCE

1 medium onion, minced
1 carrot, minced
1 teaspoon minced shallots
½ cup butter
8 ounces red wine
1 tablespoon flour
1 pint chicken broth
2 cups diced mushroom stems
4 peppercorns
3 sprigs parsley
1 bay leaf
Salt and pepper to taste

In saucepan melt butter, then add minced onion, carrot, and shallots. Sauté them gently until golden brown. Sprinkle with flour and cook a little longer. Add wine and let simmer for a few minutes. Add chicken broth, diced mushroom stems, peppercorns, bay leaf, and parsley. Cover and simmer over low flame, stirring occasionally, for 30 minutes. Strain, correct seasoning, and serve.

EGG CUSTARD
FLORENTINE COLONY

1 *pound fresh spinach*
4 *tablespoons butter*
½ *teaspoon nutmeg*
4 *slices bacon*
½ *cup grated Parmesan cheese*
8 *ounces Gruyère cheese, finely sliced*
4 *eggs*
2 *cups light cream*
Salt and pepper to taste

Preheat oven to 350°F. Cook spinach in a very little amount of salted water. Drain, cool, squeeze to remove any remaining water, and chop finely. Melt butter in a pan, add spinach, season with salt, pepper, and nutmeg and cook for 5 minutes, stirring occasionally. Butter 4 ramekins and place an equal layer of spinach in each. Fry bacon until very crisp, crumble, and mix with grated Parmesan cheese. Sprinkle this mixture over spinach. Cover with a layer of diced Gruyère cheese. Beat eggs, blend in light cream, and pour over spinach-cheese layers. Place ramekins in oven and bake for 25 minutes or until egg custard is completely set. Serves 4.

EGGS ENCORE COLONY

1 loaf firmly textured white bread, unsliced
4 tablespoons butter
2 cups Creamed Chicken Hash
4 eggs, poached
2 cups Sauce Mornay
2 tablespoons grated Parmesan or Gruyère cheese
Salt and pepper to taste

Preheat oven to 350°F. Slice off 4 crosswise sections of bread approximately 3½ inches thick. Trim off crust. With a sharp knife, make a neat incision on the top of each section and scoop out center to form a cavity, leaving about ½ inch on the sides and at the bottom. Melt butter and brush bread evenly with it. Fill each cavity with Creamed Chicken Hash. Poach eggs and place 1 on top of each chicken-filled cavity. Cover with Sauce Mornay, sprinkle with cheese, and place in oven until cheese is melted and sauce slightly browned. Serves 4.

CREAMED CHICKEN HASH

1 2-pound chicken
1 cup light cream
Salt and pepper to taste

Remove skin and debone chicken. Mince finely meat of breasts, thighs, and legs. Season with salt and pepper to taste. Blend well with 1 cup light cream.

SAUCE MORNAY

4½ tablespoons butter
4½ tablespoons flour
1 cup milk
½ teaspoon salt
⅛ teaspoon pepper
1 cup heavy cream
2 egg yolks
⅛ teaspoon cayenne
1 cup grated Parmesan or Swiss cheese

Blend butter and flour to a smooth paste. Heat milk to scald-
ing. Blend in roux;* add salt and pepper. Stir constantly
until mixture boils. Simmer for 30 minutes. Reduce flame
and blend in thoroughly cream, cayenne, cheese, and egg
yolks.

* *Equal amounts of flour and butter mixed together.*

EGGS BONNE FEMME
COLONY

1 *tablespoon vinegar*
8 *large eggs*
8 *round toasts*
8 *medium large mushrooms*
3 *tablespoons butter*
1 *tablespoon minced parsley*
Salt and pepper to taste
2 *cups Sauce Mornay*

In a shallow pan, heat to boiling point a quart of water to which you have added 1 tablespoon vinegar. Break eggs and slide on the water surface one at a time. Lower flame, simmer for 3 minutes, remove from pan with a slotted spoon, and place each egg on top of a toast round slightly larger than the egg itself. Brush mushrooms thoroughly under running water, dry, and cut into thin slices. Melt butter in pan and sauté mushrooms. Season with salt and pepper. Turn off flame and blend in parsley. Add both to Sauce Mornay. Place egg-topped toasts into a buttered, shallow baking dish, cover with Sauce Mornay, and if desired, sprinkle with some more grated Parmesan cheese, and place in a 350°F. oven for 10 minutes to brown. Serves 4.

EGGS MOLLET
PORTUGAISE COLONY

4 large ripe tomatoes, peeled
1 tablespoon grated onion
½ tablespoon sugar
2 tablespoons butter
Salt and pepper to taste
8 large eggs

Simmer tomatoes and other ingredients for ½ hour. Butter 4 ramekins and cover bottoms of each with the stewed tomatoes. Place 2 shelled soft-boiled eggs on top of the tomatoes in each ramekin. Sprinkle with freshly ground pepper. Serves 4.

EGGS WITH ARTICHOKE BOTTOMS COLONY

4 large artichokes
4 eggs
6 tablespoons Sauce Mornay
4 tablespoons grated Swiss cheese
Salt and pepper to taste

Remove stems and outer leaves of artichokes. Cut off 1 inch from the top. Boil in salted water until tender (approximately 25 minutes). Remove from pot, drain, and when cooled, with a silver knife scrape the edible tender part from leaves. Blend it with Sauce Mornay to make a smooth paste. Poach eggs and carefully place one on each artichoke bottom. Spread artichoke–Sauce Mornay paste over eggs, sprinkle with grated cheese, and place in moderate oven just long enough to warm through and let the cheese melt. Serves 4.

FISH

Fillet of Sole Monique
Salmon Kedgeree Colony
Fillet of Halibut Colony
Baked Smelts Colony
Lobster Escalopes
Fillets of Mackerel Venetienne
Lobsters Bordelaise
Glasmastarsill (Glassblower's Herring)
Stegt Rødspaette (Sautéed Flounder with Shrimp)

FILLET OF SOLE MONIQUE

1½ pounds fillet of sole (about 4)
2 tablespoons butter
2 tablespoons chopped parsley
¾ cup Chablis
¼ teaspoon salt
⅛ teaspoon pepper
8 medium mushrooms
8 oysters in liquid
1 tablespoon roux*
1 cup heavy cream, whipped

Wipe fillets with damp paper towels. In hot butter, in large skillet, arrange fillets; add parsley, Chablis, salt, pepper. Simmer, covered, 10 minutes. Remove from heat. Meanwhile, simmer mushrooms in boiling water for 5 minutes and then drain. Also, gently heat oysters in liquid just until edges begin to curl, then drain. With slotted spatula, remove fish to heat-proof serving platter. Arrange mushrooms and oysters around fish, set aside, and keep warm. Add roux to liquid in skillet. Cook, stirring until thickened. Add seasoning if needed. Pour sauce over fish and cover with whipped cream. Run quickly under very hot broiler to brown top. Serves 4.

* *Equal amounts of flour and soft butter mixed together.*

SALMON KEDGEREE COLONY

1 *medium onion*
1 *carrot*
2 *ribs celery*
2 *sprigs parsley*
2 *pounds fresh salmon*
4 *hard-boiled eggs*
2 *cups cooked rice*
2 *cups curried Béchamel Sauce**
2 *ounces brandy, heated*
Salt and pepper to taste

Place salmon in a pot with enough salted water to cover. Add onion, carrot, celery, and parsley. Bring to a boil, then simmer for approximately 10 minutes. In the meantime cook rice (⅔ cup in 2 cups water) and eggs. When salmon is cooked, remove from pot, take off skin and bones and cut into 2-inch pieces. Shell and cut eggs in bite-size pieces. Drain rice well. Drain salmon and add fish pieces, eggs, and rice. Season to taste, then add half of the Béchamel Sauce and brandy. Toss lightly, being careful not to break salmon or eggs. Heat through for a couple of minutes. Transfer to serving dish and pour over the remaining Béchamel Sauce. Serves 4.

---

* *Make Béchamel Sauce as indicated earlier in the book and blend in a teaspoon of curry powder.*

FILLET OF HALIBUT COLONY

4 *halibut fillets (approximately 1 ½ pounds)*
3 *tablespoons butter*
2 *tablespoons onion juice*
2 *tablespoons lemon juice*
¼ *cup flour*
2 *eggs, hardboiled*
2 *cups Béchamel Sauce*
2 *sprigs parsley, minced*
Salt and pepper to taste

Preheat oven to 450° F. Melt butter, blend in onion and lemon juices and enough salt and pepper. Dip halibut fillets in this mixture, then roll each over itself and fasten with either toothpick or skewer. Flour lightly, then arrange in a well-buttered baking dish and bake for 12 minutes. In the meantime, grate the yolks of the 2 eggs and cut the whites into thin strips. Gently remove toothpicks or skewers from fillets. Pour Béchamel Sauce around them and sprinkle with egg yolk, whites, and minced parsley. Serves 4.

BAKED SMELTS COLONY

2 *pounds smelts*
4 *tablespoons butter*
1 *cup dry white wine*
1 *tablespoon anchovy paste*
2 *tablespoons lemon juice*
⅛ *teaspoon mace*
¾ *cup fine bread crumbs*
Dash of cayenne
Salt and pepper to taste

Preheat oven to 350°F. With two tablespoons of butter, coat generously a shallow baking dish. Reserve 2 tablespoons of wine. In the remainder, blend in anchovy paste and lemon juice. Pour into baking dish and arrange smelts in it. Season fish with mace, cayenne, salt, and pepper. Cover with bread crumbs and dot with 2 tablespoons butter cut into small pieces. Bake for 25 minutes. Serves 4.

LOBSTER ESCALOPES

2 *live lobsters (1 to 2 pounds each)*
1 *rib celery*
1 *medium-small onion*
1 *carrot*
3 *tablespoons butter*
1 *teaspoon paprika*
2 *ounces brandy or whiskey*
3 *tablespoons cream*
Salt and pepper to taste

Peel onion, scrape carrot and celery, cut into coarse pieces, and boil in 4 quarts of salted water for 15 minutes to make a court bouillon. Plunge live lobsters into it and cook them for 20 minutes. Remove from pot and cut off tail, legs, and pincers. Cut the rest in escalope-size pieces. Heat butter in saucepan, add escalopes, season with salt and pepper to taste, and sauté for 10 minutes. Remove all meat from cracked legs and pincers, cut it into small pieces, then rub through a sieve.* Blend in paprika, brandy, and cream to form a smooth sauce. Add more cream if you prefer a thin sauce. Heat through without boiling and pour over the escalopes. Serves 2.

* *Instead of a sieve, a blender can be used for this operation.*

FILLETS OF MACKEREL VENETIENNE

4 mackerels (12 ounces to 1 pound each)
4 tablespoons butter
2 tablespoons flour
2 cups fish stock or beef consommé
1 egg yolk
1 teaspoon tarragon
1 lemon
Salt and pepper to taste

Without removing skin, fillet fish, cut each fillet in half crosswise, then place in a well-buttered shallow baking dish. Season with salt and pepper, dot with butter (approximately 1 tablespoon), cover with tight lid or aluminum foil, and bake for twenty minutes in a 350° F. oven. In the meantime, prepare a sauce by melting 1 tablespoon butter and mixing in thoroughly 2 tablespoons flour. Cook this mixture over very low flame for 3 to 5 minutes, stirring constantly. Add consommé a little at a time and continue cooking for 25 minutes, stirring frequently. When sauce is almost done, blend in egg yolk and tarragon. Correct seasoning. Remove skin from fish fillets, then transfer them to serving dish, being very careful not to break them. Pour sauce over them and garnish with lemon wedges. Serves 4.

LOBSTERS BORDELAISE

2 *live lobsters (1 to 2 pounds each)*
3 *tablespoons oil*
3 *tablespoons brandy*
2 *tablespoons minced shallots*
2 *ripe tomatoes, peeled and coarsely chopped*
1 *pint red wine*
⅛ *teaspoon cayenne pepper*
2 *tablespoons flour*
1 *teaspoon minced parsley*
Salt and pepper to taste

Section lobsters in equal pieces. Remove the coral and set aside. In a saucepan, heat oil, add lobsters, and sauté until they become red. Remove pot from burner, pour off oil, add 2 tablespoons brandy and flambé. After flame dies down, add shallots, tomatoes, and salt and pepper to taste. Return pot to burner and cook for 3 minutes over low heat, stirring gently. Add wine and a dash of cayenne; cover pot and let simmer over low flame for 15 minutes. Remove lobsters to warm serving dish. Continue to simmer liquid until it is reduced to one half. In the meantime, make a smooth paste of coral, flour, butter, and 1 tablespoon brandy. Add this mixture to the liquid in the pot and simmer for five minutes. Pour sauce over lobsters. Garnish with minced parsley. Serves 2.

GLASMASTARSILL
(Glassblower's Herring)

Pickling Liquid
¾ *cup white vinegar*
½ *cup water*
½ *cup sugar*

2 *salted herrings, 1 to 1½ pounds each, cleaned and
     scraped, and soaked in cold water for 12 hours, or
     substitute 4 canned matjes herring fillets*
1½-*inch piece fresh horseradish root, scraped and thinly
     sliced, or substitute 2 tablespoons prepared horse-
     radish, drained and squeezed dry in a kitchen towel*
1 *medium carrot, peeled and thinly sliced (¾ cup)*
2 *small onions, preferably red, peeled and thinly sliced
     (¾ cup)*
¼-*inch piece ginger root, thinly sliced (optional)*
2 *teaspoons whole allspice*
2 *teaspoons whole yellow mustard seeds*
2 *large or 3 small bay leaves*

Bring the vinegar, water, and sugar to a boil in a 1- to 1½-
quart enameled or stainless-steel saucepan, stirring constantly until the sugar dissolves completely. Then remove
the pan from the heat and let the pickling liquid cool to
room temperature.

Meanwhile, wash the herrings in cold running water
and cut them into 1-inch-thick pieces. Arrange a thin layer
of onions in a 1-quart glass jar (a Mason jar, if possible)
equipped with a tightly fitted cover. Top with a few slices
of herring, carrots, ginger root, and horseradish, and scatter

with allspice, mustard seeds, and a bay leaf. Repeat until all of the ingredients have been used, making 3 or 4 layers.

Pour the cool pickling liquid into the jar; it should just cover the contents. Close the jar securely and refrigerate it for 2 or 3 days. Serve as an appetizer, or as part of a smorgasbord. Serves 6 to 8.

STEGT RØDSPAETTE
(Sautéed Flounder with Shrimp)

4 fillets of flounder, ½ pound each
Salt
Flour
½ cup dried bread crumbs
2 eggs
2 tablespoons water
8 tablespoons (¼-pound stick) butter
2 tablespoons vegetable oil
½ pound small cooked shrimp, peeled and deveined
Lemon wedges

Plaice is the fish the Danes usually prepare in this matter, but flounder is an excellent American substitute. Danish shrimp are the 1-inch variety similar to U.S. West Coast shrimp. Choose the smallest fresh shrimp available.

Rinse the fish in cold water and dry with paper towels. Salt lightly, dip in flour and shake off any excess. Spread the bread crumbs on wax paper. In a mixing bowl, beat the eggs together with the 2 tablespoons of water, then dip each fillet into the egg mixture and coat each side thoroughly with the bread crumbs. Let them rest for at least 10 minutes before cooking. Heat 2 tablespoons of butter and 2 tablespoons of oil in a heavy 10- to 12-inch skillet over moderate heat. When the foam subsides, sauté the fillets for 3 to 4 minutes on each side, turning them with a spatula. When golden brown, transfer the fillets to a heated platter. In a separate pan, melt 2 tablespoons of butter over moderate heat. Add the shrimp and toss them in the butter for 2 to 3 minutes until well coated. Place a line of the shrimp down the center of each fillet. Melt the remaining butter over low heat until it turns a rich, nutty brown, pour over the fish fillets, and garnish with lemon wedges. (If you prefer, serve with a parsley sauce.) Serves 4.

ENTRÉES

Cream of Chicken Colony
Filet Mignon Hunter's Style
Sweetbreads à l'Armagnac
Mousseline de Jambon
Beef à la Mode
Rognons Colony
Braised Shoulder of Lamb Provençale
Duckling with Orange (Hot Orange Sauce)
Chicken Sauté Colony
Breast of Chicken Gismonda
Chicken Breasts Doria
Picatta di Pollo (Chicken Piquante)
Spinach-Cheese Dumplings (Ravioli)
Zucchini Casserole
Jansson's Frestelse (Jansson's Temptation)

CREAM OF CHICKEN COLONY

1 *2-pound chicken*
1 *medium-size onion*
1 *carrot*
1 *rib celery*
3 *sprigs parsley*
1 *quart water*
1 *quart chicken consommé*
3 *tablespoons rice*
2 *tablespoons cream*
¼ *cup Béchamel Sauce (light)*

Peel vegetables and cut into coarse pieces. Place in a pot with chicken, water, and consommé and bring to a boil. Skim liquid after it has simmered for 5 minutes. Add rice and continue cooking until the chicken is tender and the rice cooked. Remove chicken from pot, carefully separate breasts from bird, and set aside. Debone and skin the rest of the chicken and cut meat into small pieces. Strain broth and add vegetable and rice to the cut chicken meat. Run this mixture through a blender, then return to the pot and blend it into the broth thoroughly. Simmer for 10 minutes, then stir in cream and Béchamel. Neatly dice the chicken breasts you have previously set aside and add them to the soup. Serves 6.

FILET MIGNON
HUNTER'S STYLE

4 fillets
1 pound fresh mushrooms, sliced
2 tablespoons butter
6 ounces dry white wine
2 shallots, minced
1 teaspoon tomato paste
1 tablespoon minced parsley
1 cup Béchamel Sauce
Salt and pepper to taste

Melt butter in skillet. Add mushrooms and sauté until golden brown. Add shallots and cook one minute longer. Season with salt and pepper. Dilute tomato paste into wine, pour over mushrooms, and continue cooking until liquid is reduced to one half. Sprinkle fillets with salt and pepper and broil on both sides until done as desired. Remove to serving dish and serve surrounded by mushrooms. Serves 4.

SWEETBREADS
à l'ARMAGNAC

1 pound sweetbreads
2 tablespoons lemon juice
6 strips bacon
1 medium onion, sliced
2 teaspoons minced chives
1 tablespoon minced parsley
6 sliced mushrooms
2 tablespoons bread crumbs, browned
2 tablespoons Armagnac
Salt and pepper to taste

Simmer sweetbreads for 20 minutes in boiling, salted water to which lemon juice has been added (1 tablespoon to 1 quart of water). Drain. Plunge in cold water and remove membranes. Line a casserole with bacon strips, sliced onion, and mushrooms. Place sweetbreads over them and sprinkle with chives, parsley, salt, and pepper. Cover and cook in oven at 350°F. for 45 minutes. When about done, remove bacon, baste sweetbreads with pan juices, sprinkle with Armagnac and bread crumbs. Bake uncovered for 5 minutes longer. Serves 4.

MOUSSELINE de JAMBON

½ pound cooked ham
½ cup heavy cream
½ cup milk
2 large eggs
1 teaspoon minced parsley
Salt and pepper to taste

Cut ham into coarse pieces and place in a blender with cream, milk, and egg yolks. Run until you have a smooth mixture. Beat egg whites until stiff, but not dry. Blend into ham mixture, then season with salt and pepper and sprinkle with parsley. Cook in the top of a double boiler for 45 minutes. Ideal for lunch. Serves 2 generously.

BEEF à la MODE

5 pounds top round of beef
6 thin strips salted pork
6 ounces brandy
1 tablespoon minced parsley
¼ teaspoon nutmeg
1 bottle red burgundy wine
2 tablespoons butter
1 tablespoon peanut oil
Salt and pepper to taste
2 cups sliced parboiled carrots
2 cups parboiled small white onions

Marinate salted pork strips in a little brandy and lard beef with them. Sprinkle meat with salt, pepper, nutmeg, and parsley. Blend remaining brandy and wine in a bowl and marinate beef in it overnight. Melt butter in a deep, heavy pan, add oil, and when hot, add beef. Brown thoroughly on each side, add marinade and simmer, covered, for 2 hours. Remove beef to another pot, add partially cooked carrots and onions, strain braising liquid over it, cover, and finish cooking (approximately 20 minutes). Slice meat, arrange on a warm platter, and serve with its own sauce and vegetables. Serves 8 to 10.

ROGNONS COLONY

2 *veal kidneys*
6 *tablespoons butter*
1 *teaspoon minced shallots*
8 *mushrooms*
6 *ounces sherry wine*
1 *teaspoon fine type of mixed herbs*
1 *tablespoon minced parsley*
Salt and pepper to taste

Cut veal kidneys lengthwise and chop finely after removing any fat and gristle. Melt 3 tablespoons butter in a pan and brown kidneys in it lightly and quickly. Remove kidneys to hot platter. In same pan, melt the remaining butter, add minced shallots, then add sliced mushrooms and fry them gently and quickly until brown. Sprinkle with herbs, salt, and pepper and then add wine. When almost completely evaporated, blend in previously cooked kidney and cook 1 or 2 minutes longer. Sprinkle with parsley and serve immediately. Serves 4.

BRAISED SHOULDER OF LAMB PROVENÇALE

1 shoulder of lamb (approximately 3 pounds)
2 cloves garlic
5 anchovy fillets (5 to 7 anchovies)
1 tablespoon rosemary leaves
4 tablespoons olive oil
2 medium onions, sliced
4 ripe tomatoes peeled and coarsely cut
2 cups sliced zucchini
½ cup black olives
¼ cup minced parsley
Salt and pepper to taste

Have butcher bone a shoulder of young lamb. Mash anchovy fillets, crush one clove garlic, and blend together. Spread mixture over meat, sprinkle with salt, pepper, and rosemary leaves, then roll and tie with a string. Heat oil in a cast-iron casserole or skillet. Brown meat thoroughly on each side, reduce flame, add sliced onion, one minced clove of garlic, and tomatoes. Cover and cook for five minutes longer. Then, still covered, place casserole in oven and cook for about an hour at 325°F. Add zucchini, olives, and parsley and continue cooking for 10 minutes longer. Excellent accompanied by rice. Serves 8.

DUCKLING WITH ORANGE

1 duckling (5 to 6 pounds)
½ quart court bouillon
4 whole peppercorns
2 unpeeled oranges
Salt to taste

Preheat oven to 425°F. Cut off neck from duckling, remove giblets and liver, and place in ½ quart court bouillon. Simmer for 1 hour, strain and reserve broth. Fold skin of duckling's neck over back and fasten with a poultry pin. Sprinkle inside of bird with salt, then stuff with peppercorns and quartered oranges. Place duckling side up on a rack in a shallow roasting pan and cook uncovered for 30 minutes. Reduce oven temperature to 375°F. and continue roasting for an additional 1½ hours. Every half hour, remove fat from roasting pan. When cooked, carefully remove all stuffing from cavity and discard. Place duckling on warm serving platter. Serve with Hot Orange Sauce.

HOT ORANGE SAUCE

Rind of one orange
Juice of 2 oranges and 1 lemon
1 *cup duck broth*
3 *tablespoons sugar*
1 *tablespoon water*
1 *tablespoon vinegar*
2 *tablespoons Grand Marnier**

With potato peeler, remove rind of one orange and cut in long thin strips. Pour boiling water over it, simmer for five minutes, drain, and add to the juice of two oranges and one lemon. Blend in one cup of the reserved duck broth thickened with brown roux, correct seasoning, and heat without boiling. In a small, heavy pot, melt sugar to which water and vinegar have been added, and cook until it reaches a golden amber color. Blend into the orange sauce. Finish by stirring in Grand Marnier.

* *¼ cup dry sherry wine can be used as a substitute.*

CHICKEN SAUTÉ COLONY

½ of 2-pound chicken
4 ounces sliced raw truffles
⅓ cup cream
3 tablespoons Béchamel Sauce
Butter
Lemon juice
Brandy
Cayenne
Asparagus tips, cooked

Sauté chicken in butter with 4 ounces of sliced raw truffles, then remove the chicken to a dish. To the chicken drippings add ⅓ cup of cream and 3 tablespoons of Béchamel Sauce and reduce. Take from fire and add a little melted butter, a few drops of lemon juice, a few drops of brandy, a little cayenne, and some asparagus tips (cooked). Pour sauce over chicken. Serves 1.

BREAST OF CHICKEN GISMONDA

2 whole chicken breasts, boned and split to yield 4 sections
1 egg, well beaten
1 teaspoon salt
⅔ cup fine dry bread crumbs
Oil or other fat for frying
¼ cup butter
Dash of nutmeg
⅓ pound mushrooms, sliced (tops only)
2 tablespoons sherry
1 package frozen chopped spinach, cooked

Place chicken sections on cutting board and pound as thin as possible with wooden mallet or base of a heavy saucer. Dip them in egg that has been mixed with cold water. Then dip in bread crumbs mixed with salt. Let stand at room temperature for 10 minutes. Meanwhile, cook spinach according to package directions, drain, add 2 tablespoons butter and dash of nutmeg. Keep hot. Sauté mushroom slices in remaining butter for 5 minutes. Add sherry. Cover and keep hot. Heat oil in a heavy pan until a 1-inch cube of bread browns in 48 seconds. Lower prepared chicken-breast halves into it. Cook chicken pieces 5 or 6 minutes on each side, turning them with a slotted spoon. They will rise to the surface of the fat when they are done. Remove and drain on paper towels. Arrange 4 servings of spinach on a platter, with a cooked chicken breast on each. Overlap mushroom slices neatly on each chicken breast and spoon some of the mushroom pan liquid over the portions. Serve at once. Serves 4.

CHICKEN BREASTS DORIA

4 breasts of chicken
½ pound butter
3 tablespoons flour
2 small cucumbers
1 lemon
Salt and freshly ground pepper to taste

Have butcher debone and remove skin from 4 plump chicken breasts and flatten them with a wide knife blade. Lightly coat them with flour. In large skillet, melt 6 tablespoons butter. Sauté breasts until they are golden, being careful not to overcook. Season with salt and remove to a heated platter and set aside. Peel cucumbers and cut into four pieces lengthwise. Remove all seeds and dice. Add remaining butter to skillet and sauté cucumbers for 3 minutes. When cooked, spoon them over chicken breasts and season with freshly ground pepper and a few drops of lemon juice. Serves 4.

PICCATA di POLLO
(Chicken Piquante)

8 chicken thighs and drumsticks
¼ cup olive oil
1 tablespoon oregano
2 tablespoons red wine vinegar
Salt and pepper to taste

Wash chicken pieces and dry thoroughly. Arrange in one layer over oiled bottom of a shallow baking dish. Drizzle remaining oil over chicken; sprinkle with salt, pepper, and oregano. Turn chicken pieces once or twice while baking in a 350°F. oven for 45 minutes. Sprinkle vinegar over chicken and continue baking for 15 minutes longer. Serves 4 persons. Good cold as well as hot.

SPINACH-CHEESE DUMPLINGS (Ravioli)

2 10-ounce packages washed fresh spinach
1½ cups ricotta cheese
2 eggs, beaten
2 tablespoons grated Parmesan cheese
½ cup flour
Salt and pepper to taste

Cook spinach in a very small amount of salted water. Drain, let cool, then squeeze out all water by pressing repeatedly between hands. Chop. With a wooden spoon, blend eggs into ricotta, add Parmesan cheese and chopped spinach, and continue mixing until all ingredients are thoroughly blended. Season with salt and pepper. Pick up a small amount of mixture at a time, gently roll between palms into the shape of a large oblong walnut, and roll onto floured board. Have a large pot full of boiling salted water. Drop dumplings in a few at a time. Remove one at a time with a slotted spoon as soon as they come to the surface. Place in a serving dish. Top with generous amount of melted butter, more grated Parmesan cheese, and freshly ground pepper. Enough for 4 people if served as a main dish, more if served as a side dish with meat or fish.

ZUCCHINI CASSEROLE

¼ cup olive oil
1 medium onion, chopped
1 clove garlic, whole
2 tablespoons minced parsley
3 large ripe tomatoes, peeled and chopped
6 medium zucchini
¼ cup grated Parmesan cheese
Salt and pepper to taste

Heat olive oil in heavy skillet. Add first 3 ingredients and sauté until onion is golden and limp. Remove garlic. Add tomatoes. Season with salt and pepper and cook a little longer. Wash and trim ends from zucchini. Slice thinly without peeling. Alternate layers of zucchini and tomato mixture in a 2-quart casserole, finishing with tomato mixture. Sprinkle with grated Parmesan cheese and freshly ground pepper. Cover and bake in a 350°F. oven for 30 minutes. Serves 1. Equally good served hot or cold.

JANSSON'S FRESTELSE
(Jansson's Temptation)

*7 medium-size boiling potatoes, peeled and cut into
    strips 2 inches long and ¼ inch thick*
2½ tablespoons butter
2 tablespoons vegetable oil
2 to 3 large yellow onions, thinly sliced (4 cups)
16 flat anchovy fillets, drained
White pepper
2 tablespoons fine dry bread crumbs
2 tablespoons butter, cut into ¼-inch bits
1 cup heavy cream
½ cup milk

Preheat the oven to 400°F. Place the potato strips in cold
water to keep them from discoloring. Heat 2 tablespoons of
butter and 2 tablespoons of oil in a 10- to 12-inch skillet;
when the foam subsides, add the onions and cook 10 minutes, stirring frequently, until they are soft but not brown.

With a pastry brush or paper towels, spread a 1½- to
2-quart soufflé dish or baking dish with the remaining half
tablespoon of butter. Drain the potatoes and pat them dry
with paper towels. Arrange a layer of potatoes on the bottom
of the dish and then alternate layers of onions and anchovies,
ending with potatoes. Sprinkle each layer with a little white
pepper. Scatter bread crumbs over the top layer of potatoes
and dot the casserole with the 2 tablespoons of butter cut
into bits. In a small saucepan, heat the milk and cream until
it barely simmers, then pour over the potatoes. Bake in the
center of the oven for 45 minutes, or until the potatoes are
tender when pierced with the tip of a sharp knife and the
liquid is nearly absorbed. Serves 4 to 6.

SALADS

Salade à l'Italienne
Spinach Salad
Winter Salad
Salade Demi-Devil
Orange Salad
Fiesole Salad
Endive Salad
Turnip Salad

SALADE à l'ITALIENNE

1 avocado pear
1 good-sized mushroom
1 white truffle
Lettuce, white center leaves
Parsley sprigs
Olive oil
Lemon juice
Salt
Black pepper, freshly ground

Cut avocado pear in half. Remove the pit and the skin of the pear and then slice ½ the avocado pear thinly. Cut mushroom and white truffle in like manner.

On a salad plate arrange in single file a line of avocado pear, one of mushroom, and another of white truffle, with each slice overlapping the preceding slice. Garnish the outer edges of the salad plate with the white center leaves of the lettuce and small sprigs of the parsley.

For this salad, serve a dressing of the following ingredients. Use 1 part of olive oil, 2 parts of lemon juice, a liberal amount of salt and freshly ground black pepper. Mix the dressing very thoroughly and then serve by spooning the dressing over the salad. Serves 2.

SPINACH SALAD

1 10-ounce bag washed fresh spinach
4 strips bacon
3 tablespoons olive oil
2 tablespoons lemon juice or wine vinegar
Salt and pepper to taste

Rinse spinach in cold running water and drain thoroughly. Remove stems and midribs from leaves and cut in thin strips, using a sharp knife. Fry bacon until crisp, then drain off half the fat. Mix vinegar, salt, and pepper together and pour on the cooked bacon and melted fat. Pour this mixture over the salad. Toss lightly. Serves 4. Especially good with beef, veal, and broiled liver.

WINTER SALAD

2 firm, ripe pears
2 red apples
1 cup finely chopped celery leaves
2 tablespoons olive oil
3 ounces white wine vinegar
Salt and pepper to taste

Peel and core pears; wash and core apples. Dice fruit and place in well-chilled bowl. Add celery leaves. Mix oil, vinegar, salt, and pepper together and toss lightly. Serves 4. Excellent with roast pork and lamb.

SALADE DEMI-DEVIL

4 medium-size potatoes
1 truffle, the size of a large walnut
2 tablespoons olive oil
1 tablespoon white wine vinegar
1 teaspoon French mustard
Salt and pepper to taste

Boil potatoes in their jackets. When cool, peel and cut into thin slices. Cut truffle into paper-thin slices and then cut each slice into strips. Mix together oil, vinegar, mustard, salt, and pepper. Pour over potatoes and toss gently, being careful not to break the potatoes. Serves 4. Excellent with any meat and fish.

ORANGE SALAD

2 *large (preferably seedless) oranges*
2 *medium Bermuda onions*
½ *cup pitted black olives*
2 *tablespoons olive oil*
Salt and pepper

Peel oranges and cut into thin slices. Remove seeds if necessary. Slice onions, wash in cold water, and press dry between the folds of a kitchen towel. Slice olives. Place everything in a bowl. Mix oil, salt, and pepper together and pour over the salad. Toss gently. Serves 4. Especially good with roast pork and baked ham.

FIESOLE SALAD

1 cup diced boiled potatoes
½ cup diced boiled carrots
1 cup boiled green beans
1 large ripe tomato
6 large, pitted black olives
1 tablespoon capers
4 anchovy fillets
2 hard-boiled eggs, sliced
From ½ to 1 cup mayonnaise, depending on taste

First place the three vegetables in a bowl. Immerse tomato in very hot water for 2 minutes, then in cold water for another minute. Peel and dice, removing seeds. Slice olives and add to vegetables with capers and anchovy fillets cut into small pieces. Blend in mayonnaise thoroughly. Correct seasoning, adding a bit of salt and pepper if desired. Garnish with egg slices. Excellent for buffet suppers with baked ham or roast turkey.

ENDIVE SALAD

3 small heads Belgian endive
1 can sliced beets
½ bunch watercress
2 tablespoons olive oil
1 tablespoon lemon juice or white wine vinegar
Salt and pepper to taste

With a sharp knife, cut endive crosswise in ½-inch sections. Separate leaves, wash and drain thoroughly. Place in a bowl. Remove hard stems from watercress and chop. Drain beets and cut slices in half. Add to endive. Mix together oil, lemon juice (or vinegar), salt, and pepper. Pour over salad and toss lightly. Serves 4. Good with any meat and fish.

TURNIP SALAD

4 small, tender turnips
Salt and pepper
2 tablespoons oil

Choose 4 small, tender turnips. Brush thoroughly under running water and scrape with a carrot peeler or similar implement. Cut into paper-thin slices. Sprinkle with salt and pepper. Season with 2 tablespoons oil (no vinegar) and toss. Serves 4. Excellent with pork roast and baked ham.

DESSERTS

Eggs à la Neige
Beignets Soufflés (Sauce Sabayon)
Fruit Preserve Pie (Crostata di Frutta)
Mazarintarta (Mazarin Cake)
Rødgrød med Fløde (Red Fruit Pudding with Cream)

EGGS à la NEIGE

6 *large eggs*
3 *cups milk*
1 *cup sugar*
2 *pieces vanilla bean*

Separate eggs and beat whites until very stiff, but not dry, folding in ½ cup of sugar while beating. Drop vanilla beans into the milk and scald it, in a wide but not too deep pot. Remove pot from fire, dip heaping spoonfuls of egg whites on top of milk, and poach them for a few minutes on each side. Remove the egg-white "eggs" from the pot and place them on a napkin to dry and cool. Mix together egg yolks and the rest of the sugar, beating until very smooth and lemon colored. Over them gradually pour the hot milk in a thin thread, stirring constantly. Return to pan and cook until boiling point, always stirring. The mixture should thicken, but be very careful not to boil it. Strain and chill. Pour in a bowl or other deep serving dish with egg-white "eggs" floating on top. Serves 4.

BEIGNETS SOUFFLÉS

¼ cup butter (½ stick)
1 pinch salt
2 pinches sugar
⅓ cup sifted flour
4 eggs

Bring water, butter, salt, and sugar to boiling point in a saucepan over heat. Remove from heat, add flour, and stir. Return to heat, and when mixture boils again and rises somewhat in the pan, remove from heat and add eggs, one at a time, beating continuously. Drop bits of dough, each the size of a small walnut, one at a time into moderately hot deep fat. Gradually increase the heat so that the little dough-walnuts expand as they cook. When they are a deep brown, remove to paper towels. Sprinkle with confectioners' sugar.

Serve with:

Sauce Sabayon
6 egg yolks
1 cup sugar
2 cups Marsala or sherry wine
1½ ounces rum

Beat egg yolks until light and foamy. Gradually add sugar and beat until mixture has a light, creamy consistency. Add half the wine, beat, then add the rest. Continue beating this in the top of a double boiler over gently simmering water until mixture doubles in volume. Remove from heat and add rum.

Serves 4 to 6.

FRUIT PRESERVE PIE
(Crostata di Frutta)

1 ½ cups unsifted flour
3 egg yolks
1 whole egg
⅓ cup granulated sugar
½ teaspoon salt
1 teaspoon grated lemon peel
⅓ cup soft sweet butter
1 8-ounce jar coarsely cut fruit preserves (cherries,
*   peaches, or apricots)*

Put flour on board. Make a well in center. In this put egg yolks, sugar, salt, and lemon peel and mix with fingertips. Work butter into egg mixture, then work in flour a little at a time. When all ingredients are blended into a smooth paste, knead dough hard 5 or 6 times. Wrap in waxed paper and chill for 30 minutes. Cut off ⅓ of dough, then roll out larger portion to fit the bottom of a 9-inch pie plate. Spread fruit preserve over bottom evenly. Roll out remaining dough and cut into strips. Make a lattice over fruit preserve, sealing ends over pie-plate edge. Brush with beaten egg. Bake for approximately 50 minutes in 350°F. oven.

MAZARINTARTA
(Mazarin Cakes)

Pastry
8 tablespoons (¼-pound stick) unsalted butter, softened
1½ teaspoons sugar
¼ teaspoon salt
2 egg yolks
1⅓ cups all-purpose flour

Cream the butter and sugar together by using an electric
mixer set at medium speed or by beating them against the
side of a bowl with a wooden spoon until light and fluffy.
Beat in the salt and the egg yolks, 1 at a time. Now beat in
the flour and mix well. Flour your hands lightly and shape
the pastry into a ball. Wrap in wax paper and chill for at
least 30 minutes. Makes 1 8-inch round cake.

Frangipane Filling
8 tablespoons (¼-pound stick) unsalted butter, softened
1 cup almond paste, at room temperature
2 eggs, lightly beaten
1 teaspoon grated lemon rind
2 teaspoons flour
1 tablespoon butter, softened
Confectioners' sugar

Cream the butter by using an electric mixer set at medium
speed or by beating it against the side of a bowl with a
wooden spoon until it is light and fluffy. Beat in the almond
paste, 2 tablespoons at a time, and then beat in the lightly
beaten eggs. Continue to beat until the mixture is very

smooth, then stir in the grated lemon rind and flour. Set aside.

Preheat the oven to 325°F. Place the chilled dough on a floured board or pastry cloth. Dust a little flour over it and roll it out from the center to within an inch of the far edge. Lift the dough and turn it clockwise, about the space of 2 hours on the clock; roll again from the center to the far edge. Repeat lifting, turning, and rolling until you make a circle 11 or 12 inches in diameter and about ⅛ inch thick. Butter the bottom and sides of an 8-inch false-bottomed cake pan with the tablespoon of softened butter.

Roll the pastry over the pin and unroll it over the pan, or drape the pastry over the rolling pin, lift it up, and unfold it over the pan. Gently press the pastry into the bottom and around the sides of the pan, being careful not to stretch it. Roll the pin over the rim of the pan, pressing down hard to trim off the excess pastry. With a rubber spatula, spread the filling on top of the pastry.

Place the cake pan in the center of the oven for 45 to 50 minutes, or until the pastry is golden brown and the filling is set. Let the cake cool a little in the pan, then set the pan on a large jar or coffee can and slip down the outside rim. Slide the cake onto a platter, sprinkle with confectioners' sugar, and serve at room temperature.

RØDGRØD med FLØDE
(Red Fruit Pudding with Cream)

*1½ pounds fresh raspberries or strawberries, or a com-
    bination of the two (or substitute 2 10-ounce pack-
    ages frozen berries)*
2 tablespoons sugar
2 tablespoons arrowroot powder
¼ cup cold water
Slivered almonds
½ cup light cream

Remove any hulls from the fresh berries. Wash the berries
quickly in a sieve, drain and spread them out on paper
towels, and pat them dry. Cut the larger berries into quarters
and place them in the container of an electric blender. Whirl
at high speed for 2 or 3 minutes until they are puréed. If
you are using frozen berries, defrost them thoroughly, then
purée them in the blender, juices and all. To make the
dessert by hand, rub the fresh berries or the contents of
the packages through a fine sieve set over a large mixing
bowl. Place the berry purée (which should measure about
2⅓ cups) in a 1- to 1½-quart enameled or stainless-steel
saucepan and stir in the sugar. Bring to a boil, stirring constantly. Mix the 2 tablespoons of arrowroot and the cold
water to a smooth paste, and stir it into the pan. Let the
mixture come to a simmer to thicken the jelly (do not let
it boil), then remove the pan from the heat.

　　　Pour into individual dessert bowls or a large serving
bowl. Chill for at least 2 hours. Before serving the *rødgrød*,
decorate the top with a few slivers of almonds and pass a
pitcher of light cream separately. Serves 6.

INDEX